PSYCHOLOGICAL SAFETY

Original title: Psychologische Veiligheid
(Amsterdam: Boom, 2nd edition 2020).

Imprint: Independently published

Translated from Dutch by Christine Strik
Cover design: Studio Jan de Boer
Interior design and lay-out: Villa Y

© 2020 Hans van der Loo & Joriene Beks

ISBN Paperback: 9798580090412
ASIN E-book: B08QDMMGD2

All rights reserved. No part of this publication may be reproduced, stored in a retrieval system, or transmitted in any form or by any means, electronic, mechanical, photocopying, recording or otherwise without the prior written permission of the authors.

Hans van der Loo
Joriene Beks

# PSYCHOLOGIAL SAFETY

Signpost to Fearless Performance

# TABLE OF CONTENTS

**Rocking Psychological Safety** 7
– Preface by Jitske Kramer

**Introduction** 11
Safe Zone 15
The Journey Takes Off 16
To the Point and Practical 17

**1 The Secret of Successful Teams** 21
Help, Emotions! 22
Fear as an Incentive 22
Anything New is Met with Resistance 23
Why one Team Outperforms the Other 25
The Secret of Successful Teams Unraveled 26
You'll Only See it When You Get it 27
The Hidden Life of Psychological Safety 30
Big Five: Dimensions and Proven Effects of
    Psychological Safety 32

**2 Psychological Safety: Ins and Outs** 37
War Rooms without Safe Zones 38
The Abilene Paradox 39
The Fear of Loss and Change 40

Just do it 42
The Benefit of the Doubt 43
Why Strong Teams Make More Mistakes 44
'My Bad' 45
Three Golden Ingredients of Psychological Safety 46
Look the Captor Straight in the Eye 47
Even in Teams, People are Taken Hostage 49
Care & Dare 49
A Delicate Balance 53

**3  The Everyday Reality of Psychological Safety** 57
Create Positive Impact 58
Energy at Critical Moments 60
Psychological Safety in Figures 61
Psychological Safety in the Four Energy Zones 63
One Team is Not the Other 65
Chill Team 67
Fear Team 69
Race Team 70
Safe Team 71

**4  Safety Leaks and the Logic of Fear** 75
The Inventor of Safety Leaks 76
Terror Regime on the Factory Floor 77
Psychological Unsafety on the Dutch Work Floor 77
The Rise of the Scaredy-lion 80
Viral Fear: Imaginary Threats 82
The Logic of Psychological (Un)safety 84
From Big Five to Small Five 86

| | |
|---|---|
| The Use of Safety Leaks | 87 |
| Fear as a Weapon | 89 |

## 5 The Warm Way to Psychological Safety — 93
| | |
|---|---|
| Psychological Safety Can be Radical | 94 |
| Actions Speak Louder than Words | 96 |
| A Question of Authentic Leadership | 98 |
| Cold and Warm Ways to Psychological Safety | 101 |
| Change Formula for Psychological Safety | 103 |

## 6 How to Spark Safety — 111
| | |
|---|---|
| A Grip on Trust | 113 |
| A Grip on Candor | 117 |
| A Grip on Making a Difference | 121 |
| Three Flight Routes to Create *Safe Zones* | 125 |
| The Procedural Route | 126 |
| The Cultural Route | 128 |
| The Interplay Route | 130 |

## The Story of Joriene and Hans — 133
| | |
|---|---|
| Joriene's Story | 133 |
| Hans' Story | 136 |

| | |
|---|---|
| Frequently Asked Questions | 139 |
| Content-Related Questions | 140 |
| Process-Related Questions | 142 |

| | |
|---|---|
| References | 147 |
| Literature | 153 |

# ROCKING PSYCHOLOGICAL SAFETY

– Preface by Jitske Kramer,
 author of *Jam Cultures*

Safety is a notion often referred to in static and procedural terms. There are safety rules and regulations, and there are scripts, programs and safety procedures. Crew Resource Management is a method implemented in airplanes and hospitals. It means communicating and working together transparently and professionally, according to strict procedures – an efficient way to keep planes in the air and prevent medical error. At the same time, clear boundaries and protocols are no guarantee that people will feel safe to express themselves. And this happens to be an important component of psychological safety, the theme of this book.

Psychological safety cannot be achieved on cue or on paper. It reflects the form of cooperation, the working climate, the culture within groups, teams and organizations. It refers to a variety of elements, such as feeling at home in a group and feeling free to speak up when it counts, having the courage to admit to making errors, the presence of a clear and healthy power balance, being able to spitball new and differing ideas, and remaining positive, despite all the commotion that surrounds you. And to top it off, the authors of this book claim, the culture of psychological safety stems from forces that are hard-to-operationalize and that are potentially tense, such as trust, candor and the desire to make a difference. Added together, we're dealing with a rather 'messy' subject.

As a corporate anthropologist I feel right at home. The misconception that we can shape cultures simply by deploying new core-value programs is very persistent. A culture is created together – through a relentless process of pushing and pulling, inching and pinching, hemming and hawing. A process very much like a jam session in which the ensuing music is achieved through improvisation and interaction. Jamming is a tool structuring cultures, and subsequent collaboration, to really rock together. Even in organizations, it's hard to make yourself heard without someone pulling you back in line forthwith. It's equally important to show a sincere interest in others, as well as a willingness to recalibrate. To know when it's time to step out of the limelight allowing space for people who think and act differently from you. To seek synergy, where the end result is more than the sum of its parts. Just like a jam session, you play together in teams and organizations without knowing precisely where it leads. One thing's for sure: We'll do everything in our power to genuinely listen to each other in order to make a difference together. In doing so, we're able to speak freely and rock. And at times when we feel our freedom is curbed and we find it challenging to share our thoughts, we're brave enough to follow through nevertheless. Hence: Candor.

The authors of this book have succeeded in clarifying what psychological safety actually means. Moreover, what it doesn't mean. It's not a free pass for some wide-eyed group-hugging culture, as it's sometimes thought. On the contrary, as countless examples in this book will illustrate, psychological safety can be tough as nails if push comes to shove. Only to switch to being gentle and sympathetic at other moments. I often refer to it as an inclusive culture in which people collaborate assuming a powerful connection and affectionate boundaries. Another thing that appeals to me: Psychological safety is not something you need to talk about at length; it's mostly a matter of doing. Of effort. Of trial and error. Of trusting one another. But also, of demonstrating leadership. Of going out on a limb. Deviating from the sheet music. And finding your own musical patterns. This book incites us to not wait too long. Start with a first note. See who falls in and plays along. See to it that psychological safety gradually starts to rock!

   Jitske Kramer

'Don't be too timid and squeamish about your actions. All life is an experiment.
The more experiments you conduct the better.'

– Ralph Waldo Emerson

# INTRODUCTION

American Internet giant Amazon is not exactly glorified for being a warm and caring employer. It emanates a competitive and ruthless workplace ethic – all in the name of frosty figures and arctic accountability. Yet the company culture strongly encourages its people to be frank and forthright with each other. Transparency and integrity are the rule; ducking responsibilities and office politics are not even mildly tolerated. People are expected to interact candidly, to address and refute one another. To actually report errors, and subsequently put their best foot forward to learn from the experience. Sharing knowledge has become part of their daily routine; putting forward new ideas is common practice. Open dialogue is the foundation on which the company has thrived.

Founder and CEO Jeff Bezos himself can be held accountable for this. 'Be radically frank,' he's been known to say. Unlike his peers, Bezos doesn't feel the need to surround himself with yea-sayers. He's more interested in people who can advocate contrasting ideas and resourceful solutions. There's but one constraint: You must be able to corroborate anything you say; don't base your claims on a hunch or gut feeling.

## Be radically frank, is Bezos' credo

The following anecdote puts it all in perspective. During a board meeting, Bezos proudly announces that web site revenues are skyrocketing according to the new data system. Marilyn, a Manager responsible for monitoring warehouse sales and invited to the meeting as a one-off, is dumbfounded. These figures are definitely three times the real deal. While others savor the favorable turnover, Marilyn speaks up.

'Jeff, these numbers aren't right,' she says.

'They're straight from the database,' Bezos counters.

'Still, they're incorrect,' Marilyn persists.

Can she substantiate this? Marilyn gets a few documents containing warehouse data from her bag and reads them to the board. For a spilt second, you can hear a pin drop. And then everyone starts sharing thoughts about what could be the root cause. It turns out the data system derived its numbers from virtual shopping carts instead of actual purchases. The fact clients virtually stuff their shopping carts with way more items than they actually intend to buy had not crossed the programmers' minds.

And so, by putting things in focus, Marilyn instigated a quick fix.
It may seem the most natural thing in the world: Identify an issue, uncover the problem, and set out to find a solution together. And in the process, you learn how to avoid these hitches in future situations. How hard can it be? In practice however, people tend to conceal errors, or even hold back on comments. Thus keeping excellent ideas to themselves, not asking the relevant questions or simply not speaking their minds. The numbers speak volumes. American research has shown that 85% of all employees face situations where they do not feel at liberty to share their point of view. Their boss' proximity being an important aspect. But even without the boss lurking around, a lot of people choose to remain silent. And this is anything but a typical American phenomenon. More than two thirds of all Dutch employees (69%) stated they feel unable to speak frankly when the situation calls for it. Clearly the fear of freely sharing our views is considerable. In other words: The workplace feels unsafe to share thoughts candidly.

More and more often the term 'psychological safety' is applied against this background. It's the talk at conferences, workshops and seminars. Trainers, coaches and consultants consider it a new area of expertise. The graph above shows us that the subject increasingly pops up in searches worldwide.

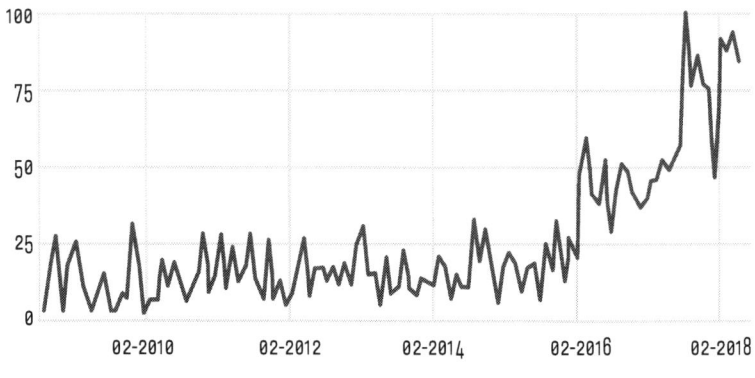

**THE GROWING POPULARITY OF PSYCHOLOGICAL SAFETY**

Source: Global Google Trends

## The fear of freely sharing views is considerable

So what exactly does the concept mean? Harvard Professor Amy Edmondson, one of the lead experts in this area, describes psychological safety as a climate in which people are comfortable to take interpersonal risks. According to her, psychological safety encompasses more than a subjective feeling. The term refers to a group trait: A climate or culture in which people feel free and safe to ask questions, dare to speak their minds, are empowered to address and refute one another, where they report mistakes and talk about them, and express concerns or propose new ideas without being asked.

## Safe Zone

Psychological safety translates into having a sense of home: You feel strongly connected to the other members of the household. You don't have to wear a mask or play-act. You are one hundred percent accepted for who you are. Psychological safety provides a safe zone similar to home, where you are free to express yourself, and from where you can explore and examine new worlds without fear of retribution. It provides a basis of connectivity and trust, of candor and authenticity.

> **Psychological safety provides a safe zone similar to home**

Oddly enough, the preconditions we take for granted at home are often not there at work. There, we allow ourselves to be led by many fears. The fear of losing face, job insecurity, of becoming the target of aggression and bullying, and not being heard. Afraid to stick our necks out or to give the boss or a colleague a piece of our mind. Fearful of being punished for mistakes, of losing a promised bonus, or not being considered fully employable. And this, maybe the ultimate fear: To be informed you're redundant or superfluous.

Psychological safety is meant to protect us from fears we come across in our everyday work life and to possibly bend them into a positive flow. Negative energy is then converted into positive energy. It enables us to join in with conversations, activities and decision-making processes at work – fully-fledged and uninhibited.

## The Journey Takes Off

Now we have sketched the rough outlines of our subject, we can set the journey in motion. What does psychological safety imply, why is it important, and what's the best way to cultivate it? We'll explore this in detail in the next few chapters.

To answer the questions, we have chosen the following buildup:

- What's the secret of winning teams? Spoiler alert! It's psychological safety. What is it, which factors prompt psychological safety, and what results will it bring? You'll read about all this in Chapter 1.

- How does psychological safety work? In Chapter 2, we'll dive deeper into scientific research on the topic to get to the very core of psychological safety.

- In Chapter 3, you'll discover how psychological safety can be quantified in Dutch organizations and in various branches. This is a chapter about psychological safety in everyday practice.

- Continuing to Chapter 4, we'll address what aggressing components munch away at psychological safety, and we'll illustrate that achieving psychological safety is harder than you might think. It allows us to demonstrate why the topic is more relevant than ever.
- Psychological safety is a collective task that flourishes with good leadership. In Chapter 5, we'll provide a warm approach and a change format to transform teams and organizations into safe zones.

- By way of closing argument, you will find numerous practical handles to spark psychological safety in Chapter 6.

## To the Point and Practical

We wrote this book as an inspirational and practical tool for executives and other professionals, for consultants, coaches and trainers. It is based on extensive studies of relevant literature and years of field experience. We made a deliberate choice to keep it short and sweet because we believe the topical theme of 'psychological safety' requires a concise and easy-access approach. You can read the book in just a few hours and get right on it. It's meant to set your mind at work and inspire you to take action. Because creating a workplace culture that's really *lit* is not the work of external consultants or trainers. It's not a boardroom 'thing'. Ultimately, you and your team decide whether your work climate is safe and inspiring enough to prosper every day.

We hope you will put the insights in this book to practice without delay, and that as of tomorrow you'll speak your mind, as well as make yourself vulnerable when the situation calls for it. That you will feel free to bombard your team and the rest of the organization with bright ideas. Before you know it, you'll spark fireworks!

'Life is either a daring adventure or nothing at all.'

– Helen Keller

# 1

# THE SECRET OF SUCCESSFUL TEAMS

Psychological safety appears to be growing into a hype these days, yet to a large part of the working population it's still a non-issue. It can even provoke downright resistance. So when we recently read a consultant explaining in a news article the importance of safety and trust in the workplace, the interview raised both approving and critical comments. 'What a load of bull!' an angered gentleman posted. 'Do you honestly believe that the people who rebuilt The Netherlands after World War II even thought twice about this kind of nonsense? Just work hard, do the best you can, and don't fool around.'

## Help, Emotions!

Exit psychological safety. But what lies at the root of this resistance? We distinguish three main obstacle drivers. First of all, we're dealing with a relatively new and vaguely-known concept. We tend to associate safety with protection against physical threats or, if you take it one step further, with transgressive social behavior. To many people, psychological safety is merely taking it one step too far. Especially when you associate it with culture and feelings. Quite a few managers consider these subjects vague and elusive. Feelings are unpredictable, and they cannot be dictated. It's kind of tricky to push people into feeling safe. However, it also holds true that people can be taught to deal with emotions, even though this may require social skills that not everyone masters.

> To many, psychological safety is just one step too far

## Fear as an Incentive

The second reason to be critical of psychological safety harks back to the notion that fear, and not so much safety, is the driving force behind performance at work. People are often classed as unwilling to work by nature, prone to laziness, and would go to great lengths to do as little as they can possibly get away with. To prevent this from happening, they need a strong hand. Don't listen to employees, provide them with clear instructions. Don't allow them space, and always be on their case. Enforcing compliance and obedience then becomes the essence of good management: 'Stop fooling around', and fear to a certain extent, seems to work. Research shows that fearful employees work harder and longer hours, and make fewer public comments about management. But this only holds true for routine operations. And only in the short term. Fear and related stress lead to a great variety of negative effects in the long run, such as making mistakes, burnouts, increasing absenteeism, steep staff turnover and performance decline. We will get to that in Chapter 4.

## Anything New is Met with Resistance

The third reason for resisting psychological safety is the most persistent. It combines a mixture of automatic aversion towards anything new, and gross overrating of one's own abilities. Sometimes, when we start to talk about psychological safety, we're awarded with a spontaneous chuckle. 'Let's not complicate things, shall we,' they will prompt. 'If I want to speak up, I will. I've never been impeded by fear of doing so.' After which the subject is quickly changed. Yet do you honestly believe there are people who actually never felt any tension when taking the floor or addressing someone? It seems hard to believe.

Who out there isn't familiar with those difficult and tense moments and the tendency to hold your tongue because:
- You felt you said something stupid
- You were afraid to slow things down
- You thought people wouldn't listen anyway
- You were insecure about other people's reactions
- You didn't want to appear defiant or an overachiever
- Or... (just fill in the blanks)

What can we learn from criticism of psychological safety? For one thing, that the concept requires further exploration. We need to define its essence through thorough research and by adding numbers and narratives. And secondly, that it is harder than we think to refute some of the superseded suppositions. For example, that fear is an effective and efficient motivator, when it's quite the opposite. And lastly, that it's not enough to spread zealous stories about psychological safety around the world without acknowledging the natural defense mechanisms in place. Initially, every new idea is met with skepticism.

Take the famous video from 1998, in which Dutch commentator Frans Bromet asks a few locals in Amsterdam about their thoughts on mobile phones. Nobody in the video has anything good to say on the matter. But, lo and behold, a few years later everyone was using the device. A hopeful thought: Even set ways are susceptible to change.

## Why one Team Outperforms the Other

Why does psychological safety deserve serious attention? Let's delve deeper into a study on high-performance or winning teams. Professor Stanley Eisenstat issued an assignment to his IT students at Yale University; he thought a whip-smart scholar should be able finish the assignment in a day. His expectations were valid. However, the slowest students took ten days to properly complete the task. The speed devils worked ten times faster than the snails! Intrigued by the outcome, other researchers carried out experiments involving teamwork. The difference between fast- and slow-operating teams amounted to a factor of forty. Based on studies of peak performances, scientists from various universities illustrated that the disparity between high-performing and under-performing teams can go from a factor of fifty to as high one hundred. In conclusion: There's more flexibility in human performance than we think.

These remarkable findings were reason enough for a group of researchers at Google to methodically ascertain the origin of these huge gaps. They based their case on performance speed, as well as other matters such as creativity, quality, learning ability, friendliness, diligence, etc. The Google team investigated no less than 180 teams, and questioned over two hundred managers, team leaders and employees. From that mountain of information, however, they weren't able to find an immediate explanatory pattern. As proper investigators do, they followed up by systematically eliminating statements put forward in other literature.

- Could differences in performance be retraced to the geographical vicinity of team members? No.
- Was it the team size? No.
- Did it have something to do with diversity within the team? No.
- Was it the youthfulness, or the opposite, the seniority of team members? No.
- Could the type of work be explanatory? No.
- How about the volume of work? No.
- Did personality traits or motives have something to do with it? No.

## The Secret of Successful Teams Unraveled

Undaunted, the team continued their research. It lead to an astonishing insight: The difference between high- and low-performance, and even downright underperforming teams can be traced back to behavior and the way they work together. Although they were now one step closer to a possible explanation of the existence of performance gaps, behavior and collaboration are quite generic and stretchable concepts. And so they diligently continued their search for a plausible explanation. Of over one hundred variables, five stood out in the end.

These were ranked according to the extent to which they influence team performance. The impact of the work turned out to be the least important aspect: Do we believe, deep down, that our work matters? Followed by the meaning of the work: Are we doing something that matters to us personally? Order and clarity – are the roles, goals and responsibilities clear to everyone – were considered a fraction more important. But this was considered to be less important than interdependence: Can we count on each other to deliver? The most important item in the line-up: Psychological safety. Described as the ability to take risks within a team without feeling insecure.

## You'll Only See it When You Get it

All the years of industrious work the research team had put in hadn't been in vain. The secret of (much) better performing teams had been unlocked. When the results were published in a big article in the *New York Times* at the beginning of 2016, it was as though a bomb had gone off. It was the talk of the town and beyond. Mostly praise, though there was some strong criticism on the study as well. Partly on scientific grounds: The research was presumed unrepresentative because the data came from one company only. A huge company admittedly, but still. A second capital sin in science: The research method they used remained, by and large, shrouded in mystery. Hence, the results were insufficiently auditable or replicable. Further critique was chiefly aimed at the practical implications of the outcome. What exactly *was* psychological safety? How could teams and organizations be made psychologically safer? Where to start? Good thing the research team had thought about the answers to these types of questions at an earlier stage. They shared checklists to establish whether psychological safety was an issue or not.

The next page shows a sample of one of these lists.

Despite all the good intentions, in practice the checklists led to more confusion rather than reducing it. For one, the sample list is mostly about things that don't take place. Opinions that aren't shared, questions left unasked, difficult or painful subjects that are avoided, feedback that isn't sought, mistakes left unspoken, and people who don't talk about their failings, or that don't even know each other personally.

## CHECKLIST:
## TO WHAT EXTENT IS PSYCHOLOGICAL SAFETY AN ISSUE IN YOUR TEAM?

How can you find out if psychological safety is an issue in your team? According to the researchers in Project Aristotle (Google), you have to be attentive to the following symptoms:

|  | TRUE | FALSE |
|---|---|---|
| There are no differences of opinion or divergent views. | ☐ | ☐ |
| At meetings, few or no questions are asked. | ☐ | ☐ |
| Difficult or painful subjects are avoided; there's a lot of pussyfooting about. | ☐ | ☐ |
| Feedback isn't provided or sought. | ☐ | ☐ |
| Mistakes aren't talked about, and when they occur, others are to blame. | ☐ | ☐ |
| Managers do most (or all) of the talking. | ☐ | ☐ |
| Peer requests are rejected. | ☐ | ☐ |
| Co-workers all know each other professionally, not personally. | ☐ | ☐ |

## The Hidden Life of Psychological Safety

In conclusion: Psychological safety leads a largely invisible and hidden life. The greater part of the issues play out under the surface. It's especially trying for managers with a 'cold-hard-facts' and 'SMART' vision. In fact, it requires a great deal of emotional intelligence – the ability to read other people's hidden emotions and handle them adequately – to uncover these hidden aspects and work on them. Awareness of what usually stays concealed is an absolute must in order to work on psychological safety effectively. To quote the late Johan Cruijff: 'You'll only see it once you get it.'

> Psychological safety leads a largely invisible and hidden life

It's never just a walk in the park, but you can develop an eye for psychological safety. To increase awareness with their managers, Google developed dedicated workshops. Participants were handed out scripts drawn from real life work scenarios with practices that enhance or reduce psychological safety.

## SCENARIO: MANAGER X IN TEAM YZ

An example. X is an experienced manager known for his technical expertise. For the past two years he's managed Team YZ, which is responsible for implementing large-scale projects. Although he's generally known to place high demands on his staff, the last few months he's been flying off the handle when mistakes are made, showing little tolerance for what he calls 'crappy ideas', and complaining about other people's performance levels behind their backs. His behavior stirs emotion with the team: The work vibe is less positive, and people are complaining more. The usual flow of new ideas is drying up. The only one speaking during meetings seems to be X. The rest are keeping their opinions to themselves and don't hold eye contact. Even outside the team, people notice something's up. A proposal submitted by X to run a new project is rejected from the top due to a lack of ambition and creativity.

Upon reading the scenario, participants are asked to explain the behavior in terms of psychological safety. Then they're asked how they would handle similar situations as a manager. What would they do to repair the climate of psychological safety? After deliberating various scenarios, it's time for self-reflection. From personal experience, which of the situations described are familiar? When have participants struggled with issues regarding psychological safety? How did they handle the situation? And what was the impact?

# Big Five: Dimensions and Proven Effects of Psychological Safety

Later on, we'll return in detail to the ways in which both awareness and skills in terms of psychological safety can be scaled up. First, we'll elaborate on the dimensions and proven effects of psychological safety. After all, Google's study led off with the question why some teams outperform others.

Once it became clear that psychological safety was the key, they dived deeper into this aspect. It led them to five dimensions and corresponding effects of psychological safety: Inclusion, addressing mistakes, input and engagement, creativity, and positivity. Together, they are what Google calls the Big Five, not to be confused with the personality theory of the same name, or the wild animals you meet on safari.

### BIG FIVE DIMENSIONS AND EFFECTS OF PSYCHOLOGICAL SAFETY

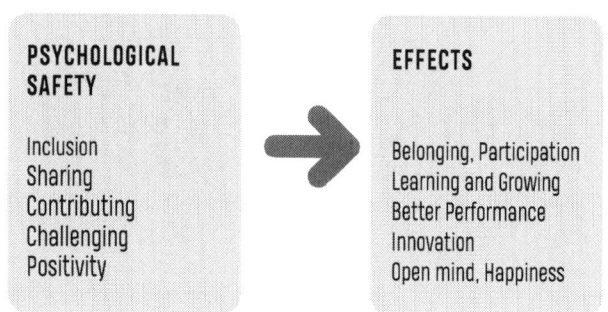

**PSYCHOLOGICAL SAFETY**

Inclusion
Sharing
Contributing
Challenging
Positivity

**EFFECTS**

Belonging, Participation
Learning and Growing
Better Performance
Innovation
Open mind, Happiness

An explanation of each dimension and its effect on psychological safety:

- **Inclusion**
  Dialogue and participation ensure positive feelings of belonging. Because of inclusion, people feel equal to others. In 'safe zones', where psychological safety prevails, people feel comfortable. They feel fairly treated and appreciated as they are. This will manifest in a high level of enthusiasm and engagement.

- **Sharing**
  Psychological safety assumes that there is openness and eagerness to learn. Opinions are openly shared. Errors are acknowledged and discussed with others. The barriers to speaking have been minimized. You honestly say what you think, address each other and discuss mistakes with each other. With the aim of learning from each other. Safe zones inspire a 'growth mindset': A development-focused and eager-to-learn stance, where people want to continuously improve themselves. This translates into the willingness to ask sharp or controversial questions, to learn new things fast and easily, to experiment, and to learn from mistakes.

- **Contributing**
  Psychological safety provides a healthy foundation to perform and deliver results. Everyone is expected to participate fully and at their own level and to make a

meaningful contribution. This ensures a healthy basis of commitment and involvement, not based on 'must' but 'want'. Employees want to add value and make a difference. Concerning the latter concept, incidentally, there are many misunderstandings. Performance is often associated with achieving targets or being bowed down by performance indicators and deadlines – all forms of competitive pressure. We are talking about the guts to take the lead, to manifest yourself, and to surpass yourself. There's no subservient component; your performance adds value and has impact on others.

- **Challenging**
  Psychological safety is a source of creativity and innovation: It encourages the propensity to challenge and shake up the status quo, to herald new ideas, to try to identify issues and propose solutions, and to come up with opportunities to change and innovate.

- **Positivity**
  Psychological safety is an antidote for negative energy in organizational teams: Fear, apathy, cynicism, egotism, fuss, intimidation, stress, exclusion, boredom, mistrust, etc. We will get back to this in detail in Chapter 4.

The Big Five: Inclusion, addressing mistakes, input and engagement, creativity, positivity

The secret of successful teams? It turns out to be psychological safety. Which, in turn, is shaped by the Big Five. The five dimensions and corresponding effects of psychological safety:

- Inclusion
- Sharing
- Contributing
- Challenging
- Positivity

Consider whether or not you recognize these five dimensions within your own team or organization.

'Safety is
not a gadget
but a state
of mind.'

– Eleanor Everet

# 2

# PSYCHOLOGICAL SAFETY: INS AND OUTS

One day, we were asked to observe a CEO and his team during a strategy session. The day started off quietly. Most of the team members came in 15 minutes to half an hour late. A few muttered some half-baked excuse, but the majority went straight to their seats without so much as a word, after leisurely grabbing a cup of coffee. An external Future Analyst, who was asked to put the team on edge, appeared to liven things up a bit: Plenty of questions were asked and opinions were shared. After the speaker left, the team set to work. It was not easy. Even though the room had been transformed into a veritable 'war room' by a communications agency – the CEO had copied this from companies like Apple, Uber and Google – the zeal to go to war on the status quo was practically non-existent.

The short-lived vibrancy during the presentation seemed to have vanished into thin air. Frustrations grew as the day wore on. Not least with the CEO, who had kept at bay most of the day under the guise of not obstructing the team. Yet what he saw during his intermittent rounds through the war room far from met his satisfaction. He wanted an innovative growth strategy, but only got more of the same. Save a few details, everything remained as it was. An experienced manager himself, he felt something was brewing within the team and he couldn't quite put his finger on it. After the session and closing drinks, he shared his frustration and asked what we'd observed over the course of the day.

## War Rooms without Safe Zones

Our answer was quite simple: We had witnessed a team that doesn't feel safe. The day had made painfully clear that no one really felt prompted to take the lead. This sense of languor wasn't caused by a lack of intelligence or energy, as they were abundant. The team didn't feel like a *safe zone* in which co-workers had the courage to discuss cutting edge topics without constraint, to learn from past mistakes and propose new ideas. Everyone was wary. Afraid to offend others. Afraid to stand out from the crowd. Afraid to become the victim of imaginary or real reprisals. So, they were on autopilot. No risky, innovative business, but more of the same. After all, what had proved beneficial in the past, couldn't hurt in the future. Or so they thought. The vibrant discussion after the lecture was merely for show. When it really came down to it, everyone started pussyfooting around. The relief of making it through the day unscathed was evident from the animated conversations during drinks afterwards. There was a lot of chitchat about all kinds of things. Except for that full-sized elephant in the room: Strategic innovation.

## The Abilene Paradox

We've pretty much all attended sessions where no one spoke their minds, and everyone switched to autopilot unintentionally. In management ideology, this has even been given a name: The Abilene Paradox. In 1974, management expert Jerry B. Harvey wrote an article on the subject. It starts with a visit to his in-laws on a heavy, hot summer day. Everyone is gathered on the porch of a house somewhere in Texas. Total boredom is looming when the father-in-law gets up and proposes a drive to Abilene to go out for a meal. Most welcome the idea. Some dread the long journey – the town is 55 miles down the road – but do not mention it because they want to keep the peace. The ride is dusty and takes forever. The restaurant is noisy and jam-packed. And to top it all off, the quality of the food is questionable. Four hours later, on the way back home, the air is thick with tension. To lighten the mood, someone declares the trip was still kind of worthwhile. The others disagree. Deep in their hearts, no one really wanted to travel to that town. Even the one who suggested it in the first place says he only did so because he thought the others were bored. Everyone joined a trip no one really wanted.

The Abilene Paradox relates to a phenomenon known in social psychology as group conformism: In a group, we easily adapt to the majority opinion. We don't openly share what we think about something, but play along and playact. If the outcome is disappointing, we don't address the author, but suffer the hardship passively and taciturn. Only when the mood in the group changes, will we come out and venture to say what we actually thought all along. Even though the term hadn't been brought to life yet at the time, this is a pure example of the primal mechanism of psychological safety. People remain silent because they don't feel safe for whatever reason to go against the mainstream opinion.

## The Fear of Loss and Change

Opinions that aren't shared. Feedback kept inside. People who don't hold each other accountable. A tale as old as time. Yet, unfortunately it happens all too often. In families as well as at work. Now, over a decade after Harvey's findings, academia is taking an interest in the topic.

# Besides fear of loss, people strongly detest uncertainties

The first one to expressly write about the concept of psychological safety is cultural psychologist Edgar Schein, affiliated with the Massachusetts Institute of Technology (MIT). He places the notion in the context of human fear of change and learning new things. In his book, *Organizational Culture and Leadership*, he highlights the emergence of a sense of insecurity that comes with change. According to Schein, it's perfectly understandable that (some of) the staff will subsequently experience feelings of anxiety. In times of transformation, the cards are reshuffled and dealt differently. The chance of not being among the winners but with the runners-up is very real. People would literally rather do anything else than lose the cards they currently hold.

Besides fear of loss, people strongly detest uncertainties and disturbance of the existing order as a result of change. It violates a sense of safety. The reaction: Resistance to change and sticking with the old as much as possible. Just like the team that didn't get much further than rehashing old ideas during their strategy day. The question is whether fear of change is as universal as Schein seems to suggest. He nuances his stance by emphasizing on imposed change. People are willing to change, he says, but they don't want to *be* changed.

In organizations, we mostly deal with imposed changes. Coming from leaders who want to appear ambitious and decisive, or who want to leave an exceptional legacy – meanwhile duping employees. But even without a decisive boss, changes are enforced in organizations. Often owing to external aspects: The economy is down, the government is proposing cuts in your sector, or a new technology that throws the market into a radical spin, even possibly turning away customers.

## Just do it

In later publications, Schein also places the concept of psychological safety into a learning perspective. As with change, feelings of fear and insecurity are common in a context of learning. Just think of the first time you were on the high dive or that awfully steep ski slope, your shaky legs moving you towards a situation that feels unusual and unsafe. The cheers from the sideline – 'don't be afraid, you can do it' – hardly get through to you. Your brain is focused on one thing only: Survival! There is but one thought: Move away from the danger! Better safe than sorry. Eventually, most people manage to rid themselves of this anxiety and indulge in learning new skills. How? Simply by doing, says Schein. Just jump off that diving board and go down that slope. Just trust your abilities, and count on others to be there just in case. All you have to do is go to a state of mind that protects you from all harm, like a shield. The name of that shield: Psychological safety. In addition, Schein recognized the positive effects of psychological safety. In his view it leads to connection and ensures focus on common objectives.

## The Benefit of the Doubt

His colleague William Kahn, a Management Professor at Boston University, directs his research on psychological safety specifically towards the work floor: What are the circumstances for co-workers to commit to, or contrary to that, detach themselves from, work? In 1990, he wrote an article in which he names psychological safety as a source of involvement and inspiration ('engagement'). According to him, co-workers benefit from less supervision and more trust. Psychological safety allows for the latter.

In this respect, Kahn speaks of awarding the other person the benefit of the doubt. Instead of the negative image of man adopted by classical management gurus – that it's human nature to be lazy and disinclined to work – Kahn is the advocate of a more positive human ideal. He assumes people are essentially decent. Given space, they will be more motivated and perform better. Psychological safety ensures co-workers show more of themselves.

## Why Strong Teams Make More Mistakes

Is this assumption actually correct? A question a young Harvard scholar struggled to answer. Her name: Amy Edmondson – also featuring in our introduction. She would become one of the leading figures in the new science of psychological safety, even though Edmondson herself accidentally stumbled across this field of research. As a student, she was involved in a medical field survey. The ultimate purpose of the study was to identify factors that explain how one team causes more malpractice and the other less. The hypothesis being that a solid and well-functioning team makes fewer mistakes. For six months, Edmondson and her fellow students collected and analyzed the data. Surprisingly, the results fully contradicted the initial supposition. Well-functioning teams made more mistakes, not less. Ill-functioning teams did the exact opposite: Their work was almost flawless. Go figure!

The research team developed a new hypothesis: Well-functioning teams do not necessarily make more mistakes; however, they are more likely to come clean if they make them. An interesting thought. How to go about finding out whether it sticks? The only way was further research with a wider variety of teams. From teams in which relationships were close and people communicated very openly, to teams that ran a tight ship and where people hardly had the guts to address one another.

This additional research showed that well-functioning teams indeed make more mistakes as they report their mistakes more openly. Members of such teams feel safe and supported enough to admit their failings. They even consider it a perfect opportunity to learn and grow. Weaker teams show the exact opposite. In those teams, the fear to bring up errors rules. They are secretly swept under the carpet. Everyone goes out of their way to show the world the 'goodie two-shoes' version of themselves. The festival of error doesn't fit that profile, so it's swept under the rug.

## 'My Bad'

Expressing yourself freely or putting yourself in a vulnerable position and talking about errors are topics often associated with personal features or individual traits. Based on her findings, Edmondson categorically disagrees with this. She claims Psychological safety primarily has nothing to do with characteristics or skills. It requires a climate in which people have the guts to take interpersonal risks. In such a climate they feel free to speak to their bosses without being told off. You can ask purportedly stupid questions without immediately being considered incompetent. Playful and innovative ideas can be ventilated readily, without the originator being put in the corner like a child. You are at liberty to talk about your mistakes without becoming the target of scorn and ridicule.

Makes sense, doesn't it? The figures and experiences (highlighted in the next chapter) tell a different story. A considerable majority doesn't always feel comfortable enough to speak their mind. In most cases, rebutting the boss is a no-go. At night, many lay awake fretting about whether or not they did the right thing and how some dire issue that is still 'on their plate' should be handled. No spontaneous feedback. Each word is measured on a golden scale. There's much at stake: Collaboration with others, their perception of our expertise, the impact on our ego. It's not unthinkable to fall flat on your face, on top of being regarded an utter fool. Or worse still, being excluded by the group. In a climate of psychological safety, these risks can be minimized and steered in a positive direction.

## Three Golden Ingredients of Psychological Safety

We've given you an idea of what can happen when a team doesn't feel safe. And even in the best of families, people sometimes don't have the guts to tell the truth. Let alone what happens in teams or organizations under pressure. Edmondson's research shows the necessity to speak our mind and own our mistakes. People who do not face mistakes, do not learn. And those who do not learn, don't perform.

Let's take it a step further. What are the ingredients required to cultivate a climate of psychological safety? Compare it to the ingredients you need to bake cookies. Without flower, butter and sugar, you won't get very far. You need all three. The same goes for psychological safety. A psychologically-safe climate emerges when the following three ingredients are accounted for: Trust, candor and the drive to make a difference.

## Look the Captor Straight in the Eye

To find out how that works exactly, we sidetrack to the unsafe territory of hostage crises. What would you do if you come face to face with a screaming and confused captor who had grabbed a random woman and stuck a knife to her throat, threatening to kill her? Shouting his head off that you're next? Someone who knows better than anyone is George Kohlrieser, an American-born clinical and organizational psychologist and Professor at IMD, a prestigious school based in Lausanne, Switzerland. He assisted the police countless times as a hostage negotiator, and was taken hostage himself on a number of these occasions. Kohlrieser wrote several books about his experiences and is a keynote speaker on the subject. He concentrates on the relationship you have to build under pressure and in a very short time to de-escalate the situation and change the captor's mind. Faced with death, you need to stay calm and display nerves of steel, *and* engage the captor. Because 'bonding' is the key factor in ending hostage situations successfully.

> **You need a sense of security to have the guts to face the uncertainty of the new**

How does he build such a bond? By looking the captor straight in the eye. By asking questions to find out as much as he can about him in a short span of time. Every human being is unique, Kohlrieser knows, and is driven by specific incentives and personal experiences.

In the case of the confused captor, it turned out soon enough that he needed to talk to someone. He answered the barrage of questions with measured replies. Little by little, the atmosphere became more positive. Once contact was initiated, Kohlrieser worked his way to what he calls a 'tipping point': The moment the captor acknowledges that it's better to stop as his fate can only get worse. 'Would you want your kids to remember you as a murderer?' was the question Kohlrieser once asked, heralding a defining moment. The captor fell silent and burst into tears. Minutes later, he surrendered.

## Even in Teams, People are Taken Hostage

You might not see it at first glance, but Kohlrieser asserts there are remarkable similarities between what happens during hostage negotiations and what you can encounter in teams. Even in teams, people are taken hostage. Sometimes by others, by an authoritarian manager for instance, but mostly by their own assumptions, speculations and personal interpretations of people. By acting on them, they keep themselves from making a difference and achieving their potential.

How can this be prevented? By building a basis of trust – which he refers to as a 'secure base' – to fall back on. If you take risks, you need to have a safe haven. Such a safe zone can consist of one or more persons, meeting points, work methods, goals or objects that offer protection. One of the key components of a safe zone is the level of interconnectivity and trust. In a safe zone, people have bonded and built trust. Cultivating an environment that offers that kind of security is one of the most important leadership challenges.

## Care & Dare

Kohlrieser is a man who takes the lead and makes a difference. He helps save hostages. To do this, he pays attention to trust and candor. Besides creating a safe zone ('care'), it's all about taking interpersonal risks: Raising your voice, addressing others, suggesting new options, admitting mistakes. And about the inspiration to explore new things as a team ('dare').

One cannot exist without the other: You need a sense of security to have the guts to face the uncertainty of the new. Leaders capable of building safe zones ensure connectivity and trust, candor and the collective ambition to make a difference. Psychological safety is thus cultivated by a mix of the three golden ingredients trust, candor and making a difference.

*Trust Dividend or Trust Expense?*

In our view, trust is the self-chosen willingness to treat the other based on positive expectations. Described as such, trust doesn't rely so much on unwavering laws of nature ('natural trust') or axiomatic conventions ('social trust') but rather flows from an authentic choice. When you trust someone, you assume that person is consistent and true to their word. Hence, authenticity and trust are closely linked.

As soon as we feel someone is wearing a mask or playing games with us, trust is out the door. And not without consequence. According to Steven Covey Jr. – indeed, son of – trust can always be translated in material or immaterial dividend. When people trust one another, collaborations run smoother and successes are greater. When trust turns

## THE THREE GOLDEN INGREDIENTS OF PSYCHOLOGICAL SAFETY

### PRECONDITIONS

Trust
Candor
Making a Difference

### PSYCHOLOGICAL SAFETY

Inclusion
Sharing
Contributing
Challenging
Positivity

### EFFECTS

Belonging, Participation
Learning and Growing
Engagement, Better Performance
Innovation
Open mind, Happiness

into mistrust, all good intentions are called into question, feelings of mutual frustration emerge because commitments aren't met, and there's suspicion about what the other person is up to. The dividend of trust will then make way for the expense of trust.

### *Candor based on self-confidence*

Self-confidence is a specific form of trust; it's all about the positive expectations you have regarding your own performance. Self-confidence refers to faith in our own abilities. When you have faith in yourself, you believe you can get things done. Self-confidence is the very source of the second ingredient of psychological safety: Candor.

It represents qualities like 'honest', 'frank', 'open-minded' or 'forthright'. And also 'using freedom of speech'. If you're candid, you feel autonomous. Unlike a pawn moved around the game board, you're able to influence the game. You have freedom of choice. You choose your own objectives and work methods. You determine your own views. And you convey them candidly.

> Self-confidence is the very source of candor

*Making a Difference: Not the Easy Route*
The third ingredient is about what you do with your performance and the impact you have. Making a difference refers to higher ambitions. Those who want to make a difference, don't choose the easiest path. They'll do anything to achieve something extraordinary and leave their mark on the world.

## A Delicate Balance

The balance between the three ingredients is in constant flux, partly due to internal influences. This can lead to a climate of psychological safety, but just as easily make it disappear. One incident, hurtful comment or angry look can be enough to make you feel unsafe; increasing pressure coming from outside, for example. When trust, candor and the desire to make a difference have been built up over a long period, then there's usually not much of an issue. The 'psychological-safety dividend' can take a punch.

One YouTube video nicely illustrates this. During a lunch concert at the Amsterdam Concertgebouw starring the famous conductor Riccardo Chailly and the equally celebrated pianist Maria João Pires, the latter suddenly appears panic-stricken when she realizes the piece they have started to play is different from the one she anticipated. Nearly in tears, with the orchestra already well on their way, she tells the conductor she didn't bring the right sheet music. Consequently he doesn't even flinch, continuing to direct the orchestra towards the piano solo. He then calmly voices a few words of encouragement to the pianist: 'You played this piece last season, you've got this.' The pianist then continues to play her solo without a single mistake. At the end, a thunderous applause ensues. A shining example of how the three ingredients combined to prevent an embarrassing outcome. The confidence bestowed by the conductor, the pianist's guts to shine without a music score in front of her, and the joint willingness to make a difference regardless, stood at the heart of a spectacular performance. Kohlrieser couldn't have done it better himself in one of his hostage crises.

> To cultivate the Big Five – and with it a climate of psychological safety – you need three ingredients: Trust, candor and the drive to make a difference.
>
> To what degree do these ingredients exist in your team or organization? And in what proportions?

'If everyone is thinking alike, then somebody isn't thinking.'

– George Patton

# 3

# THE EVERYDAY REALITY OF PSYCHOLOGICAL SAFETY

What do you do when you realize you're unable to start the demo of a promising new software product to a room full of potential buyers because of a foolish oversight on your part? 'I was in a state of utter panic,' Christal remembers. 'I knew how important this meeting was for our start-up team. We had all been fully committed to preparing for this presentation to go well. As soon as I opened my laptop, I realized something was wrong. In my haste, I had overwritten the final version with a previous beta version. My laptop screen showed… nothing. Nada. Zilch.' While the first unsuspecting participants slowly started to arrive, she broke out in a sweat and her mouth became dry as dust. Emotions ranging from anger to disappointment and desperation flashed through her mind. At the same time, she felt ashamed of her own incompetence.

## Create Positive Impact

Fortunately, she was able to share her misery with a couple of team members close by. Though shocked, their response was of understanding. Martin, with whom she had worked almost 24/7 recently, suggested she talk to Marissa, the Team leader, who also happened to be present at the time. Marissa listened attentively while Christal poured out her story almost in tears, and she tried to calm Christal down. 'It's an unpleasant situation, but such errors can occur,' she said. 'Let's see what we can do to save the day and maybe even benefit from it.' The entire team gathered round and went into solution mode. Fast forward and a plan was hatched to regain control of the situation. Marissa would first explain to the audience what had happened. Christal would then showcase the beta version with a promise to present them with the live version at twelve sharp the next day. Those who weren't interested in a virtual presentation could set up a face-to-face meeting with Christal. Owing to swift mediation, everything worked out fine. Even better than expected. The audience understood what was going on and listened more intently than ever. Christal answered numerous questions from the floor *and* received compliments for how she had overcome her setback. On her part, she set out to deliver on her promises and make the deadline of the final presentation. The team pulled an all-nighter, and the product was ready to go live at 9AM the next morning.

> A safe zone is never
> an end in itself,
> it is a means

Every team will go through moments where things don't work out according to plan. When you're surrounded by a team that works as a safe zone, chances are you will overcome adversity by coming up with constructive solutions. In a safe zone, people work together and for one another. They feel safe enough to expose themselves and speak openly about their fears and shame. They will try to calm each other down when negative emotions are causing havoc. They will encourage each other to turn every drawback to their favor. Because in the end, that's what it's all about: Creating a positive impact. A safe zone is never an end in itself, it is a means to an end. And it's all about what you do with it.

## Energy at Critical Moments

Psychological safety can be considered a source of positive energy. People who feel safe, do not worry about uncertainties, they display more positive energy and perform better than someone who is all knotted up and highly-strung. That's a proven fact. But what is energy? Energy is everything *and* nothing all in one. It's like oxygen. You need it to stay alive, but you never really stop and wonder about it. It's there. What it is and how it works, we don't know. Even though it's actually pretty simple. We'd characterize energy as the force you use to set yourself and others in motion to create the desired impact. So energy is more than a sensation. It's a force inside you that you can reveal to the outside world. That force can take shape physically, and is then called vitality. It can portray a mental state, when we focus on goals or show self-discipline. Energy of an emotional nature expresses positive or negative sentiments. And it can be a social format, when we feel connected to others and work closely together with them. Energy doesn't stand on its own. It's always connected to behavior and motion. And these are related to the positive impact you aim for. If you have low expectations, the impact will be negligible. In that case, you don't need as much energy. If you aim for the stars, you should maybe ask yourself where you're going to pull up the energy to get there. If you want to move mountains, you need piles of energy.

> **Psychological safety has a proven effect on positive energy and performance**

## Psychological Safety in Figures

Back to the evidence that psychological safety demonstrably effects positive energy and high performance. Strangely enough, in the Netherlands, there are no statistics available on psychological safety in teams. Therefore, we decided to peruse our own EnergyFinder database of more than 35,000 respondents in search of hard facts. Using Amy Edmondson's repeatedly validated survey design *Measure of Psychological Safety*, we were able to construe a *Psychological Safety Index* (PSI) representative of the working population of the Netherlands. Assuming possible ratings between 0% (zero psychological safety) and 100% (optimum psychological safety), we concluded the following (ranking from low to high):

For a better understanding: The percentages refer to the number of working people that (fully) agree with the statement. Translated into report figures, these findings does not yield a rosy picture. Contributing, Challenging and contributing to a positive atmosphere all score insufficiently. Giving your opinion freely and talking about mistakes is a taboo for more than two thirds. The free-spirited character that is often attributed to the Dutch apparently does not show itself in the workplace. Other notable scores from the survey: 53% indicate that they are not sure that others undermine you. Faith in others, ultimately, is not particularly large: The threat of others undermining your endeavors seems genuinely

**RANKING THE WORKING POPULATION IN THE NETHERLANDS ON PSYCHOLOGICAL SAFETY (2020)**

| | |
|---|---|
| Inclusion | 63% |
| Sharing | 36% |
| Contributing | 48% |
| Challenging | 56% |
| Positivity | 52% |
| | |
| Psycholgical Safety Index: | 51% |

Research done by EnergyFinder.nl among 25.000 workers

present. Asking co-workers for help scores below average. Fortunately, the last three statements are (just) above average. Evidently, And 41% say it is not easy to ask others for help. On the other hand, 67% do not reject others because they are different and that 70% say they feel safe to take risks. Added up and divided by seven, the index average is 51%, which shows that psychological safety is not doing all that well in the Netherlands. Moreover, the index figure has dropped steadily since 2014. Back then, the average was 66%.

## Psychological Safety in the Four Energy Zones

Another way to put the current index figure in perspective is by studying the coherence between psychological safety and positive energy. To demonstrate correlation, we distinguish four different energy zones.

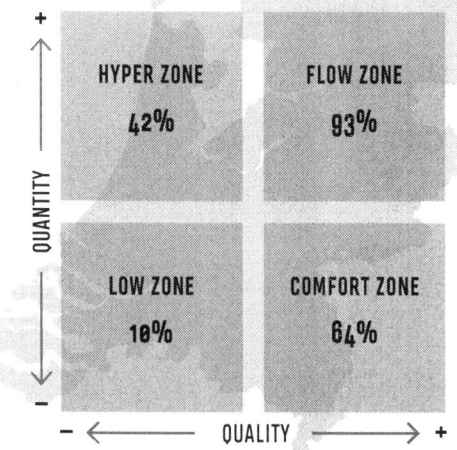

Source: Research on behalf of EnergyFinder.nl

- The Flow Zone (top right in figure below), where positive energy is abundant. People are full of confidence and work from an intrinsic motivation to deliver high levels of performance.

- The Comfort Zone (bottom right), where a positive vibe may prevail, but the people are less than vibrant. There is mutual trust, but candor and the desire to make a difference only exist to a very limited degree.

- The Hyper Zone (top left) is characterized by regular outbursts of energy, be it in an often-negative atmosphere. Mutual trust is scant, candor is sizable, and the desire to make a difference is limited to expediency.

- The Low Zone (bottom left) is dominated by low and negative energy. Trust, candor and the desire to make a difference are non-existent.

Linking psychological safety to the four different zones, we see staggering results:

In the Flow Zone – where trust, candor and the desire to make a difference are abundant – the index figure for psychological safety is 93%. This means the Flow Zone is a *safe zone*. Though much lower, the average in the Comfort Zone (64%) is still on the plus side. It's also considerably higher than the national average. The latter is not valid for the two remaining zones. The Hyper Zone (42%) and the Low Zone (10%) rank substandard and significantly lower for psychological safety than the national average.

When teams get overstrained as a result of work pressure or other circumstances and end up with Hyper-zone energy levels, or when they shut down completely and end up in the Low Zone, it's code red for psychological safety. Time for rapid intervention. However, don't jump to conclusions based on averages. We come across teams in the Comfort Zone and even in the Flow Zone where psychological safety leaves a lot to be desired. We should also hasten to say that it's often a snapshot. A few short and sweet interventions are usually enough to clear the air for the team to get back to work in their safe zone. To understand how these interventions work, we take a look behind the scenes of four types of teams.

## One Team is Not the Other

One is not the other. And even one team can be different from time to time, as the energy zones illustrate. We adjusted the figure on page 67 and linked it to the extent to which the three golden ingredients of psychological safety are present. The vertical axis is unchanged: Low energy at the bottom and high energy at the top. The horizontal axis has been modified, with the left displaying a low score on the three golden ingredients, and a high score to the right. On the left side a lacking and on the right an existing climate of psychological safety. Interlinking both axes provides a matrix in which we can distinguish four types of teams, each with their own distinctive form of psychological safety.

Psychological safety can and must not be reduced to a personal issue. It's a collective task. A key component of team and organizational energy.

## TEAM TYPES AND THEIR LEVEL OF PSYCHOLOGICAL SAFETY

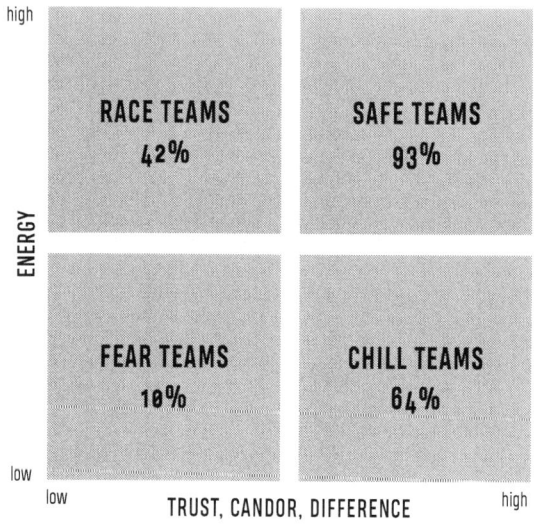

Let's zero in on the four types and their corresponding forms of psychological safety. We will start at the bottom right, with Chill Teams, and go clockwise.

*Chill Team*

Just your average project team in a somewhat rigid and rusty organization: The Chill Team, as we'll call it for now. This team emanates indolence. It starts with employees giving the company's Scrum Method a twist of their own. What's familiar is copied; what's new, like the daily stand-ups, is done half-heartedly. The daily ritual is turned into a weekly meeting ('more than enough') and they only share what everyone has planned, not what they've actually completed ('too confronting and unbecoming of our culture'). This team is not one to fulfill great ambitions. Just do what you have to, that's enough. Stories of how changes can make a difference are perceived in relative terms ('very corporate, but not our cup of tea') or cut short ('don't even start, there are too many changes on our plate already').

The team oozes serenity. There's a pleasant and relaxed atmosphere. Twenty minutes into a meeting, people still leisurely come in. Not a care in the world; everyone's busy sharing their next holiday destinations anyway. This team knows each other through and through, and their mutual trust is significant. Stability is key. We notice this when one day Team Leader John is absent. No one knows his whereabouts. However, because he'd said he had some urgent matters to discuss, they decide to wait for him, in jest trumping one another with wit about what Jan-Willem is about to share with them. When he arrives about half an hour into the meeting, he's totally oblivious. Urgent matters? As far as he's concerned, there are none. The team members casually laugh it off and decide to get some more coffee first. It may appear a mockery, but it happens: Inwardly-focused Chill Teams may well have the best intentions, but they will never go the extra mile. The mood is relaxed and everyone's on the best of terms. No one worries too much about what goes on in the outside world or about what others may have to say. Psychological safety? They've never given it a thought. They all get along nicely, and that should be enough. Right?

Explain this in terms of psychological safety and you'll see that inclusion here is mostly a question of having been with the team for a considerable time. Newcomers simply must adapt, such is the general conviction. If you don't, you'll automatically get to know the less pleasant aspects of the Chill Team. Raising your voice is hardly necessary in their eyes. Most team members are as calm and introverted as their surroundings. You won't hear them say anything too strange. Address failings within the team? Uhm, why should we? Just set up a one-on-one with your colleague and case closed. Easy-peasy.

*Fear Team*

Case examples of sketches from 'The Office', do they actually exist? Absolutely. Only in practice the atmosphere is less fun than TV producers made it look. We're visiting a team of facility engineers at a corporate multinational. Despite successive restructuring, the team has managed to get off scot-free so far. Cynically, they've labelled it a 'miracle'. They're not interested in what tomorrow brings. A cloud of fear hovers over anything new and anyone from outside the team. Especially managers from the head office – referred to as the 'Asylum' by the team – who they rather see out the door than in. When they come upon them in a meeting, there's a negative and sultry vibe. The team members sit around listlessly. People from headquarters are parroted and told unequivocally they cannot even begin to understand. There's no confidence that it'll get better. 'Some day, the hatchet will come down on this team, and that'll be the end of us,' a team member reveals.

When asked if he's ever thought of giving his work a positive spin, he looks flabbergasted. Through the years, he's unlearned to want to make a difference. 'Those people at the Asylum just make it up as they go along,' he claims. 'And we're basically toast.' When we ask the full team the same question, the atmosphere turns sour. 'No one really appreciates what we're doing. Nobody will ask us anything. Nobody takes us into consideration.' They've kicked the habit of fighting it. Instead of sharing their thoughts and feelings candidly, they've dodged towards resigned apathy and inertia.

*Race Team*

Vroom, vroom! Move away, step aside – the Race Team is approaching full throttle! If the previous teams were primarily sedate and apathetic, the Race Team is about to burst with energy. Everything and everyone is frantically caught up in work. New threats lie in wait at every corner, and there's always another fire to put out. No time to stop and think. It's all about taking action. It's all about speed, quantity and force. Targets met are immediately followed by the next.

All this energy may be contagious at first. But look closer, and you'll see the climate is grimmer than you think. There's no lack of candor; everyone shares what's on their minds. This team's interactions are tough and confrontational. A little bit of macho and macha. There isn't much time to explain, and confusion is met with rolling eyes. Other people's perceptions on all this are none of their concern. There's no time for social stuff. Everyone is busy surviving. Individual projects are prioritized. There's no shortage of frustrations and strife. Everyone gossips excessively. No stone is left unturned to vilify opponents, who are invariably labelled as 'losers'.

The Race Team is about zealous competition. It's only usually called 'healthy' by people who were able to survive. Others think differently. They're afraid of becoming the target of torrents of abuse or bullying. They are having a hard time dealing with blunt behavior that's considered normal. They don't feel safe in a climate where uncurbed frat-house behavior is combined with a shortage of mutual trust and a lack of the will to make a difference in the long run.

### *Safe Team*

And then there's the Safe Team. Did we end up in a team of 'goodie two-shoes', where everyone knows one another through and through, and there's room for personal expression? Where people choose idealist objectives to make the world a better place without a moment's hesitation? Not likely. Up close, a Safe Team is not only buzzing with energy, but ambition is decisively high. The conformism we've seen in the previous three teams, has completely vanished.

> **In the Flow Zone, trust, candor and the desire to make a difference are abundant**

The Safe Team consists of headstrong naysayers, rebels and killjoys. They don't leave things as they are, but try to come up with new and improved ideas all the time. Despite an individualistic and somewhat 'nerdy' disposition, members are closely connected. Everyone is unique, and no one receives preferential treatment. They know how to empathize with others. Out of pure conviction and pure expediency. Because in the turmoil of the outside world, as they know, you won't make it on your own. Ultimate performances are achieved by working closely together with others.

Is there room for improvement in terms of psychological safety in a well-oiled Safe Team? It might sound a little strange, but it's precisely this type of team that isn't satisfied with the status quo. They tend to never look down at those who are not performing so well; they're always looking up for inspiration on how to improve their performance.

> How does energy impact the three ingredients for a climate of psychological safety: Trust, candor and making a difference? It's reflected in different types of teams: Race Teams, Chill Teams, Fear teams and Safe Teams.
>
> Which types do you recognize within your own organization? And how about your own team?

Our deepest fear is not that we are inadequate. Our deepest fear is that we are powerful beyond measure. It is our light, not our darkness that frightens us most. We ask ourselves, 'Who am I to be brilliant, gorgeous, talented, fabulous?' Actually, who are you not to be?

– Marianne Williamson *(Our deepest fear)*

# 4

# SAFETY LEAKS AND THE LOGIC OF FEAR

The study of high-performance teams at Google from Chapter 1 reveals that psychological safety is a determining aspect of team performance. In Chapter 2, we illustrated academia's take on the topic, including its coherence with three ingredients: Trust, candor and making a difference. In Chapter 3, we saw how it pans out in practice. Even though there are plenty of positive exceptions, the *overall* image wasn't all that great. There are considerably more Chill, Fear and Race Teams than Safe Teams. We will outline why this holds true in this chapter.

## The Inventor of Safety Leaks

Building safe zones is harder than you might think as you're nearly always dealing with leaks: Negative forces that undermine psychological safety. To illustrate how these safety leaks work, we invite you to the United States East Coast. In 1899, a few million tons of iron bars lay waiting on the massive factory terrain of the Bethlehem Steel Company. They had been piled up over the previous years after the price of pig-iron took a nosedive. Now prices were skyrocketing again as demand grew, the bars needed to be lifted onto train wagons to be sold posthaste. Heavy and relatively mindless work: One laborer would lift the bar weighing over forty kilos off the stack, carry it up the ramp, chuck it in the flatbed, and walk off the ramp to repeat the process. Nobody gave efficiency a second thought. Nobody except Frederick Winslow Taylor, founder of the modern take on management, whose mission it was to maximize the prosperity of work processes. Using exact measurements and evidence-based analyses, he endeavored to figure out ways to perform better and faster, paying close attention to the quality of his workmen. The difference between highly suitable folk and the rest, he stated, is at least as big as between 'good draught horses and donkeys'. In order to assess to what extent performance could be boosted, he selected a super-strong laborer who – in Taylor's eyes – 'was mentally slow and smart as a donkey.' Doubling his salary, he encouraged the laborer to work four times harder than usual, instructing the man to do precisely as he was told. 'When you are told to pick up a bar and load it, then you will do so. And when you are told to rest, you will sit and rest. And you will do so without complaint.'

## Terror Regime on the Factory Floor

What drove Taylor initially was a deep mistrust of workers. He didn't think very highly of the human race. He thought them to be stupid, lazy and prone to all sorts of malice. Control them, and crack the whip if need be, was more his motto. He wasn't very keen on candor. Workers needed to know their place, which was at the bottom of the social ladder. God forbid they should start to think when they're here to do, never mind have a say or weigh in on decisions. Taylor saw his modern management approach as a way to improve the world. Efficiency was the magic word, and everyone needed to submit to it. Making a difference didn't mean people could handpick what goals to pursue. Nope, everyone should pull together; the manager would point them in the right direction.

## Psychological Unsafety on the Dutch Work Floor

Over one hundred years have passed since and you'd think these principles and practices would no longer exist. Working, nowadays, is supposed to be all about being happy and self-development, and not about a prevailing state of rampant fear. Aren't we at work because we like what we do, and we want to pursue our passions? Government encourages an active labor market. Companies make all kinds of efforts to optimize the 'sustainable deployment' of working people. Initiatives to boost 'work satisfaction' and transform the workplace into a 'happy culture' even take it a step further. If you read HR manuals, you'd think we are living in real-life working paradises these days. Yet safety leaks are still powerfully present.

## Even in today's working paradise, safety leaks abound

Journalist Jeroen van Bergeijk went to work undercover at a Bol.com 'Fulfilment Center'. The distribution hub was governed by a strict management approach: Do as your boss tells you. Right at the entrance, life-size signs warned about a 'zero tolerance' policy. The exit was through body scanners only. 'Security' would poke and prod sandwich bags, open cigarette packs, and even wallets wouldn't escape meticulous inspection. On the work floor there was strict hierarchy, expressed in the colors of outerwear. Bottom of the ladder (more than 90% of all employees) dressed in black. Bosses could be identified by their red fleece jackets. The pecking order was clear-cut: Up top, you give the orders and monitor the work; down below, you do as you're told. Personal initiative was not appreciated. When Van Bergwijk suggested a smarter approach for a specific action to a higher-ranking person, he was snapped at. 'You are here to execute and not to think,' is what he was told. Frederick Taylor couldn't have said it better himself.

Is this a one-time occurrence or a structural development? Sadly, it appears to be the latter. You need only look at the psychological safety indexes. And the image is confirmed in the Scientific Council for Government Policy's recent paper called 'Opting for Better' (*Het betere werk*). According to the study, we succeed at collaborating well and productively in the Netherlands, but we are also Europe's frontrunner when it comes to anxiety and aggression at work. Partly because colleagues or managers make for an unsafe workplace. Intimidation, bullying, sexual harassment and physical violence are the type of unwelcome behavior that 16% of all employees experience from co-workers or superiors. People with a migration background, especially first generation, suffer most. One in five has to deal with discrimination. Clients, patients, customers, and passengers exhibit extremely undesirable behavior even more often: A quarter of all employees in the service branch experience intimidation, harassment or unsolicited sexual attention. Public sectors such as health and welfare in particular are adversely affected. Because many professions now feature a service component, people working in the private sector also face increasing pressure and aggression from customers.

## The Rise of the Scaredy-lion

Ever more frequently, you hear about organizations stuck in the throes of a 'culture of fear'. Companies, banks, government departments, executive agencies, healthcare and educational institutions, the army, the police, universities, hospitals, sports disciplines: They have all been exposed in the media at one time or another with alarming reports about a prevailing culture of fear, sometimes even more than once. In some cases, this culture of fear is embedded in their methodology. Following in Frederick Taylor's footsteps, quite a few organizations availed themselves of a policy of fear. Feelings of anxiety and unsafety are then deliberately and systematically fueled by management in order to enforce obedience, loyalty and productivity on the work floor. And fear becomes an *extrinsic* motivator to command obedience and performance.

Some managers master the techniques to instill fear to perfection. These 'scaredy-lions' – mostly driven by their own fears – are known for their authoritarian behavior. Scaredy-lions often demonstrate irritable and erratic behavior. They treat others according to a deeply-rooted mistrust, display strong narcissistic traits, and possess little empathic abilities. They position themselves at the top of the pecking order, feel far superior to others, and want to come across as firm and decisive. They are inclined to take credit for success and to pin failure onto others. Thoroughly detesting 'mushy business', scaredy-lions prefer to surround themselves with an army of yea-sayers. At least *they* won't try to pull the rug from under their feet or argue, but facilitate the scaredy-lion's scare tactics. Thus creating scaredy-cats.

> Scaredy-lions – largely driven by their own fears – are known for their authoritarian behavior

Things can get pretty out of hand. Screaming or groping colleagues. Hurtful, insulting or derogatory comments. Cheating and stealing. Emotional outbursts. Physical and verbal threats. Sexual harassment. Systematic bullying, exclusion or retaliations. More subtle sources of social anxiety are silent treatments, being curt, badmouthing others or gossiping behind their backs, non-verbal displays of discontent, not taking any responsibility and dodging at critical moments, actions that are essentially self-serving, no timely warnings of things going south, focusing on smartphone or laptop throughout meetings, not addressing one another about unwelcome behavior (and not tolerating reprimand), coming in late without an apology, ignoring suggestions, forgetting agreements, frequently reversing decisions, selectively sharing information, unfriendly behavior, making contradictory demands, etc.

## Viral Fear: Imaginary Threats

When all these social sources of fear are relatively easy to identify and recognize, it's a lot more difficult when you're dealing with mental anxiety issues. Fears that have settled in people's minds. Sometimes based on real dangers, but most of the time on imaginary threats.

An example. A project team is visited by the Board of Directors. The team has gone the extra mile to make it a successful meeting. Not least because they have heard through the grapevine that the visit is related to a budget review. But somehow the session is not succeeding. The executives come across blunt and disinterested. The CEO leaves the meeting – allegedly to his regret – because something's up elsewhere in the organization, leaving the project team in his wake, insecure and in despair. For several weeks, gloom hangs over the group. The more they think about it, the more convinced they are that the team will face severe budget cuts. The analyst who attended the session, asks the CEO in question what's going on. In turn, he's genuinely caught unaware and taken by surprise. The reason for his lack of interest? There were numerous worries on his mind that day, on top of not having slept well the night before...

Imaginary threats are based on assumptions and speculation. They're about feelings of anxiety that settle in our brain like an invisible virus, only to take command of our doings from there. Don't be fooled – such a process starts as a tiny speck but can grow into an epidemic of huge and sometimes even catastrophic proportions, and its effects remain visible for a long time to come. Then, psychological unsafety is the product of a host of smaller microprocesses that take place between the ears.

Subconsciously, we assess whether to do something or not every time we interact with others. In a sense, we estimate whether or not we trust others and if we really want to make a difference at lightning speed. Based on this assessment, we choose, mostly subconsciously, whether or not to take interpersonal risks. As such, processes are not, or are hardly, perceptible; we often think they're of no consequence. Unjustly so. Almost one hundred years ago, American sociologist William Thomas wrote: 'If men define situations as real, they are real in their consequences.' Loosely interpreted: What you think, is certain to happen. If you feel safe, you will act accordingly. If you are in a culture of fear, you'll be careful not to take any risks.

## The Logic of Psychological (Un)safety

Fear knows many types and sources. It can emerge following acute threats. It can spread like a slowly smoldering peat fire. Later we'll outline why fear is such a persistent phenomenon. But first we need to take a closer look at how fear works. What does the logic of psychological unsafety look like? To this end, we will pivot back to the three ingredients: Trust, candor and making a difference. The absence of one or more of these ingredients, as this would implicate, leads to a decline of psychological safety. Let's see how it looks in practice.

### *From Trust to Mistrust*

Trust is about expecting others to work based on positive intentions and to do what they say. Trust can be broken in various ways. Other people can make for unpleasant surprises because they behave contrary to expectations. This can be either a one-off occurrence or structural. Mistrust can be anchored in a person's system. It can originate in a situation where a tight ship is suddenly run, as a result of a crisis situation or management changes. The very opposite – leaving things to run their course – can also lead to uncertainty and a loss of confidence. Radical changes can violate trust as well. Broadcasting that everything needs to change will send shivers down many a spine.

### *From Candor to Dodging*

Candor can be under threat from psychological unsafety. For instance, when people's input and personality aren't recognized and/or acknowledged. When you don't get any response to any of your manifestations. Or when others counter with a mocking glance or stinging mockery. Of course, candor is also the first out the door when everything is so hermetically sealed there's no room to breathe. Another reason candor is impeded: Customers, patients, clients or civilians who cross the line, airing their grievances about the service or care they've been provided. There's no shortage of criticism, especially towards industries that have lived through years of cutbacks and have been stripped to the bone – think of healthcare, welfare, education and law enforcement. Faced with physical or verbal aggression, quite a few professionals will want to curl up and disappear and abandon their professional candor. Instead of candidly voicing their opinions, they will say what angry customers want to hear, or hide behind bureaucratic procedures and processes.

## *From Making a Difference to Tailgating*

The third ingredient, making a difference, doesn't fare too well under the influence of fear either. The pressure to perform has only increased over the years. With many negative consequences to show for it. Performance pressure rarely comes hand-in-hand with more resources, meaning many employees have less time to do their job well. Let alone make a positive difference. The fear of the stopwatch and complying with mediocrity rule over once-exalted professional ideals. The rise of 'digital reputation algorithms' is an extra source of insecurity. On the surface, these virtual customer reviews are supposed to be objective: The customer expresses his or her opinion according to a number of stars or thumbs. In reality, these mechanisms are less objective than they seem. Angry customers misuse them to vent their frustrations. The fact that only the customer is given a voice through this medium and not the employee, leads to a feeling of losing control and puts extra pressure on staff members. Instead of sticking their neck out and trying to make a difference, they will keep a low profile. In that sense, it's not that different from Taylor's age.

## From Big Five to Small Five

When trust, candor and making a difference change to mistrust, dodging and tailgating, the balance of psychological safety will shift towards psychological unsafety (see figure). We fall into anxiety, apathy, and switch to autopilot. Not the Big Five from Chapter 1, but this Small Five will rule: Exclusion, mediocrity, rigidity, choosing the easy way out and negative behavior.

## The Use of Safety Leaks

So, what is the use of safety leaks that leads to feelings of anxiety and unsafety? Why can't we just live and work without them? The answer is actually pretty simple: The world is full of threats and danger. Anxiety and unsafety are a natural reflex. Whether or not deliberately, they guide us to avoid and battle the hazard we feel. This makes fear a fundamental and powerful survival mechanism.

The social law that illustrates just how powerful our anxiety is the 'Rule of Four', describing how anxiety impacts us four times more than positive feelings. It also explains the media's systematic preference for bad news. Or why even the most adulated individual can go completely off the rails when confronted with criticism. It explains why a notorious cretin can severely ruin the entire mood within a team. People are simply hardwired through evolution to chiefly pay attention to negative triggers. In psychology, this is known as the 'negativity effect'. Do we have to beat ourselves up about our coding? Not at all; it is what is it is. Without anxiety mechanisms, we would not have survived evolution.

## Fear as a Weapon

So actually, anxiety is a natural part of our lives. Yet a certain taboo seems to hover over the concept in organizations. This is partly due to the (self) image of managers, who exist by the grace of the idea that they keep things under control based on facts and insights. Talking about irrational fears quite simply doesn't fit the profile. It would only suggest there are issues at hand and that they are not on top of everything.

The unwillingness to address the topic is also related to the average manager knowing full well that fear is a powerful tool. Fear can be useful in a wide variety of situations. And

# THE LOGIC OF PSYCHOLOGICAL UNSAFETY

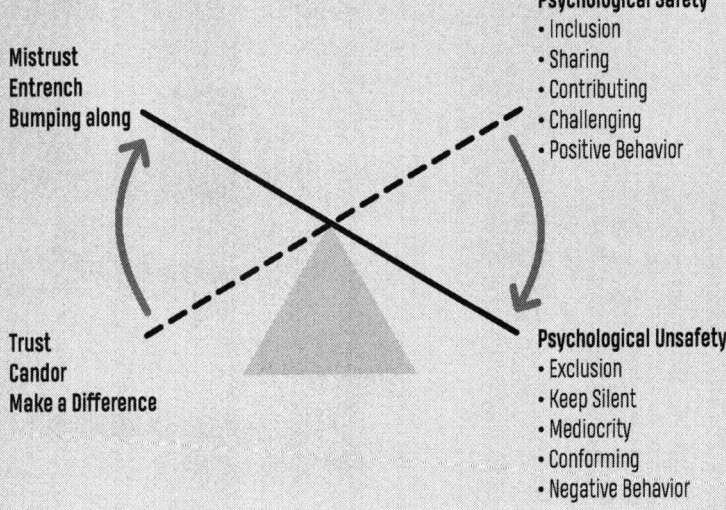

because fear is such a powerful survival mechanism, it sets things in motion almost immediately. Hence, it can be necessary from time to time to make people face the facts or to outline the image of looming doom to them. If you feel unsafe, you work harder and longer hours, and comment less on management (publicly). Threats are often an easy way to make people do their jobs; there's no time or energy wasted on the challenges of maintaining healthy relationships with employees. One well-placed command and you're done.

However, there's a dangerous catch: Fear only works in the short run. In the long run, this course of action is disastrous. Fear and stress lead to apathy and people switching to autopilot. Motivation and commitment decline, innovative capacity drops, errors go unreported and are left unaddressed, absenteeism increases, burnouts increase, and performance curves fall.

> **Fear only works in the short run**

This situation is best avoided by cultivating a climate of psychological safety. How to succeed, and together? We'll divulge it all in the next chapter.

## PSYCHOLOGICAL SAFETY

> Fear and unsafety are a natural survival mechanism in a world full of threats. They help us in imminent danger. However, to succeed in the long run, a solid climate of psychological safety is required in order to confidently and candidly direct all your energy towards a positive collaboration and make a difference together. That's why it's essential to recognize and eliminate safety leaks.
>
> What safety leaks can you identify from practice?

'If the conditions are wrong, and we fear our leaders, we are forced to spend our time and energy to protect ourselves from each other. This weakens the organization. When we feel safe in our organization, we will naturally combine our talents and our strengths and work tirelessly to face the dangers outside and seize the opportunities.'

– Simon Sinek

# 5

# THE WARM WAY TO PSYCHOLOGICAL SAFETY

Psychological safety cannot exist without trust, candor and making a difference. But there's more to it than that. Psychological safety is a multi-faceted phenomenon. It varies from one moment or situation to another and is brimming with paradoxes. Cultivating a climate of psychological safety is therefore harder than we might think. What's more, there are aggressive and contagious safety leaks on the prowl at all times.

Besides, the work on psychological safety is never done. Every time you think you've reached that perfect situation you were going for, it simply slips through your fingers. Working on psychological safety requires continuous improvement and learning at all levels. Following Professor Edmondson, we already pointed out the importance of the interpersonal level. Psychological safety can and must not be reduced to a personal problem. It's a collective task. A crucial component of the energy of teams and organizations.

## Psychological Safety Can be Radical

To everyone's surprise, the Google study of the origins of high-performance teams all pointed towards psychological safety as the main contributor. The company took this insight to heart in their own way. For one, they go out of their way to scout talents that fit their cultural profile. If you apply for a job at Google, a milling marathon of interviews awaits you. Work-contract decisions aren't made by individual managers or team leaders, but by management committees to thwart nepotism, cloning and personal blind spots. Once you're in, you're considered a full member from the get-go. You're allowed access to all the company secrets and success formulas. And you're expected to speak up from the first moment you walk through the door. Even if that means defying the top dog. Just like his Amazon colleague Bezos, CEO Larry Page is contradicted gladly. He sees debate as a productive way to get to the best possible solution and *truly* collaborate. Which includes taking a punch as well as doling them out.

## Working on psychological safety requires continuous improvement and learning at all levels

In its early years, Google was locked in a fierce battle with its much bigger and handsomely-financed competitor, Overture (don't be alarmed if the name doesn't ring a bell). Google engineers worked all hours to develop AdWords. Eventually, this would become the advertisement engine and cash cow of the company. But back then, it was no more than a faulty application. One day, Page wrote on a white board in giant words: 'These ads suck.' An engineer from another team, who had nothing to do with the tool, read the code and started working on it uninvited. He toiled for days to fix the system errors and perfect the advertisement engine. He even worked weekends. Monday morning at 5AM, without anyone having the slightest clue, the perfect tool was finished. Was the engineer aware of his heroic deed in hindsight? Nope. He couldn't even recall the incident. It was only when he was told the details that his eyes lit up and a simple 'Oh yeah' slipped out. Why wasn't his achievement etched in his brain? Because performing is everyday practice in Google culture. And because psychological safety means you help one another when push comes to shove. Uninvited. And without having to be hoisted on any shoulders.

These types of stories about psychological safety in practice illustrate that it's anything but some wide-eyed group-hugging culture. The Google culture is aimed at fast growth based on hard facts, demonstrating that behavior that's on par with psychological safety is many times more effective. Survey upon survey tells us that psychological safety benefits people and their performance. It stimulates learning abilities, contributes to stronger engagement, ensures a healthy flow of creative ideas, and leads to considerably better performance. A psychologically-safe climate is not a comfort zone in which to sit back, relax and enjoy the ride. On the contrary.

## Actions Speak Louder than Words

In fact, even exemplary companies can still get it quite wrong in terms of psychological safety in practice. An experienced Google manager recounts in an online article the story of a young and talented programmer. In an attempt to show off his best side, he blundered big-time. The system even went down momentarily, which is very similar to a deadly sin at Google. Thank goodness an experienced colleague stepped in and the flaw was remedied within a matter of minutes. Afterwards, during the weekly 'post-mortem' meeting, shortcomings of the previous week were addressed and dissected in detail. Out of the blue, the manager just flew off the handle. He bellowed it's unacceptable that inexperienced rookies venture out to make incremental improvements on their own. Raising his voice, he addressed the youngster as an 'irresponsible loser'. Everyone kept their mouth shut. No one was keen on becoming his next victim. When the employee left the room, his face drooped in dismay. What got to him wasn't so much the earful his superior gave him, but the fact that no one spoke up for him when it happened. Silence implies consent. And that's what bothered him. After a few more run-ins with his superior over the next weeks, he broke and threw in the towel. The team stood by in silence. 'It was like a scene from *Silence of the Lambs*,' he would later say. By not speaking up and letting their manager do as he pleased, the team also had to share their responsibility in the matter. And what to think of the organization? At that level, they were probably so blinded by intentions carefully committed to paper that attention for what was happening in practice was poor. A mismatch between professed values ('psychological safety is crucial') and everyday practice ('the manager calls the shots'). Candor was in short supply. Team members curled up in hiding. The monkeys didn't hear, didn't say and didn't speak. Though the article didn't mention it, the logical consequence is that they also didn't *want*. When trust and candor are lacking, the will to perform and make a difference are usually scarce. And vice versa.

## A Question of Authentic Leadership

Ensuring a climate of psychological safety is often harder than assumed. Even in organizations classified as 'safe', the degree of safety can differ from team to team. No one has an absolute monopoly on wisdom. And yet someone has to take the lead. The true essence of leadership. We feel obligated to dwell on this: It's a widely-used, though frequently misunderstood and underrated term. Google the word 'leadership' and you will get no less than 830 million hits. The number of books on the theme has run up to a hundred thousand or more. But this doesn't make it any easier to agree on the key elements of the concept. So before zooming in on the role of leadership in psychological safety, we will focus our attention on what we consider the essence of leadership.

> Psychological safety has nothing to do with a wide-eyed group-hugging culture; it's all about fast growth and efficiency

The etymological origin lies in the Anglo-Saxon word '*laed*', meaning 'pathway' or 'route'. The verb '*laeden*' refers to 'travel'. Leaders walk in front, pointing the way to their fellow travelers. They set the tone and have the courage to take risks. Leaders determine the vibe, provide a framework, and create the conditions for others to unlock their potential. Well now, there are plenty of people at the top who display very limited leadership skills. They will give directions, but only because they have the power to do so, not because they possess the trust or know-how to inspire. Inversely, people with no position of power whatsoever can prove to be great leaders. Think of examples like Gandhi, Mandela or Martin Luther King: 'Informal leaders' who inspire people to make a difference, and who create safe zones where others can realize their dreams and develop their potential. Just like home, where the leaders – we call them 'parents' – offer their children a safe haven where they can develop and grow. Extending the parallel, we see that the form of parenting can vary according to the situation. When children are young, it looks different compared to when they hit puberty. The basic ingredients of leadership *and* parenting, however, remain the same: Connecting, creating a secure environment, ensuring others (employees, children) are encouraged to take risks candidly so they are able to make a difference, now and in the future.

The authors of the one hundred thousand or so volumes about leadership often provide you with x-amount of steps to have you crowned a great leader within z-number of weeks. Don't fall for it. Leadership is not a 1-2-3 gimmick. Effective leadership means you are all-in, the whole kit and caboodle.

We call this 'authentic leadership'. Authenticity represents the feeling you're all right. The feeling of being appreciated for who you are and what you do. It also refers to the ability to be 'in line' with yourself, to acting from your core being. You're not worried about what others say or do. You are who you are. What you see is what you get. Why are authentic leaders better at cultivating a climate of psychological safety? Because authentic leaders are reliable in everything they say and do. Because they inspire confidence. And because authentic leaders are frank and forthright. They will share their opinion freely, and address other people's words and behavior. They will do so genuinely and credibly. Making authentic leaders a textbook example of candor. Besides reliability and credibility, there's a third aspect: Authentic leadership results in better team performance. Authenticity allows you to leave a footprint. To be recognized and make a difference.

True leaders, then, put their heart and soul into team relationships and performance. They are able to create safe zones in which employees feel appreciated and comfortable. Where people feel safe to express themselves. Where they can work together unconstrained. Or – if need be – can discuss and release tension.

## Cold and Warm Ways to Psychological Safety

To optimize psychological safety, you should focus on learning new behavior – and with that, unlearn old habits. Such an exercise requires a 'warm' method instead of the usual 'cold' approach consisting of systematic and top-down change programs rolled out in organizations. The instruments of choice often look well thought out and solid enough. Performance indicators irrefutably point out what needs to be done to implement change successfully. The lead time is set. Inadequate skills and abilities are passed on in large-scale training sessions, portraying it as merely a question of pushing the right buttons to get there. It sounds too good to be true. And so it is. When it comes to changing human behavior, you can put your money on this method to fail.

You can prevent this from happening by choosing a warm method. This approach is all about human behavior, from start to finish. It's about human imagination, about energy and enthusiasm, about ambitions and interpersonal relationships. In this method, changes do not run a course from A to Z. There's plenty of room for experimenting and learning. No step-by-step changes, but small interventions ('leverages') that have a major impact. The warm approach is less directive and predictable. It comes in waves. Like the swell of the ocean: Up and down, back and forth. A warm approach requires embedding and active participation. To bring new ideas to life and to make the desired difference. The signature differences between the warm and cold methods are summarized in the chart below.

### COLD AND WARM CHANGE METHOD

| COLD APPROACH | WARM APPROACH |
|---|---|
| Organization-wide Objectives | Self-imposed Team Objectives |
| Rational Analyses | Animated Visualizations |
| Overall Plan | Inspiring Subject |
| Fixed (and Long) Lead Time | Flowing (Short) Cycles |
| Focus on Manageability | Focus on Flexibility |
| Fixed Roles | Varying Ownership |
| Focus on Solving Problems | Focus on Realizing Progress |

Certainly, for people who are used to thinking along the lines of the cold approach, the warm way comes off as somewhat haphazard. But when you look at it closely, it works well and truly according to fixed patterns and systems. You'll see that scientific methodology and tested tools are at work.

The methodology we use is based on the theoretic work of American researchers James Prochaska, Carlo DiClemente and John Norcross, based in turn on years of scientific study. During the nineties, these three endeavored to unravel what works and what doesn't by systematically going through thousands of studies on behavioral change. A time-consuming job that led to a beautiful thing: A phased change method enabling the accelerated and improved realization of behavioral and cultural change.

## Change Formula for Psychological Safety

Relative to psychological safety, this methodology can be captured in the following 6S formula:

### SAFE = (SEARCH + START + SEE) X (SPEED UP + SPREAD + SET)

This equation can serve as your guide to facilitating psychological safety in your team or organization effectively and systematically. You can go through it as an individual or as a team. To give you an idea of how it works, we will walk you through the six components of the formula one by one.

- **Search**: It always starts with some legwork in an attempt to map out the current situation and the need to do 'something' about psychological safety. What is the state of psychological safety, in our opinion? And how do we measure up according to the facts? In which of the five dimensions of psychological safety do we rank highest, what are the visible shortcomings, and where could we be going terribly wrong? How can we interpret the outcome? What causes can we think of, and what patterns should we recognize?

Make sure you don't get too caught up in assumptions and subjective opinions in this phase. Try to work as an investigator or researcher would. In a sense, you are coloring the picture of a situation. It starts with what's going on. Free of judgement. Purely observing, like a window cleaner looking in and witnessing what takes place. Should you question your findings, take your time to dig deeper.

- **Start**: Once your image is complete, dip into your emotional brain. If you don't start the motion, everything will remain the same. So you have a choice. Is the situation okay, or not bad enough to require change? Then you should opt to keep doing what you're doing. If the situation doesn't feel okay, assess what you want to change, what you want to let go of, and which new paths to explore. Try to answer the following questions for yourself:
  - What would we like to change?
  - Do we want to work on mutual trust?
  - Do we want to encourage candor in people?
  - To what extent are we out to make a difference?
  - What triggers your enthusiasm the most?
  - What can be a successful first step to improve psychological safety?
  - Which successes would you use as a mirroring tool?
  - Do you have any concerns?
  - Are there any elephants in the room?
  - And what fears trouble you?

The last three questions are not meant for you to fall into gloom. This start-up phase is actually meant to find the bright spots and embark on this change process in a positive light.

- **See**: You now have a rough idea of what you want, but what does that look like precisely? Grandiloquent catch-all terms like 'authenticity', 'trust', 'candor' or 'making a difference' draw attention, but you have to use your own colors and materials to bring them to life. You can do this by building an image of the desired situation: Visualization. Create an animated and inspiring video or storyline of how you want to operate in the future. What does the future actually look like when you collaborate in a psychologically-safe environment?

After this, you can reset your brain to its rational mode to create a concrete 'design' of the desired situation.

- What behavior patterns are crucial to ensure psychological safety will improve significantly?
- At what critical moments should you ideally display the desired behavior?
- How do you convey this to others in a clear and meaningful way?

This phase mostly concerns what we want and what we can do.

- What are our strengths, and how did we use them to achieve demonstrable and durable success in the past?
- How can we optimize our strengths?
- What are the relevant weaknesses within our group?
- What behavior and skills do we master proficiently?
- How can we compensate our weaknesses as much as possible, without losing our strength?

The answers to these questions will lead to a graphic image of the desired situation and a roadmap – a colored canvas – to arrive at the desired destination. Plus, by answering the questions, you increase belief in your own abilities. A big change in itself.

- **Speed Up**: If you are already familiar with the process, you can go through the first phases fairly quickly. At the very least, quicker than formulating a business case. However, the first three phases are absolutely crucial for the change to succeed. According to research, you miss about half the change potential if you skip them. Just so you know.

In the end, it's all about acting quickly of course. Try not to take giant leaps right away, always start with small steps so you will gain experience and self-confidence in the process. Preferably take these 'micro steps' one at a time. Don't try to change multiple things all at once; focus on that one thing you think is vital. Only when you've made this into a habit, can you move to the next phase.

**TIP**: Don't merely focus on the right thing, also choose the correct moment. When pressure is high and you have a thousand-and-one things on your mind, it's better to hold off on your change plans. But make sure procrastination doesn't become the thief of time.

- **Spread**: After the first successful steps, it's time to embed and intensify. By embedding we mean: Find people who support you in your endeavors to change. You will undoubtedly run into moments of adversity and weakness. It helps if you surround yourself with people who you trust so you can candidly share your concerns and reservations, people who are just as driven to make a difference as you are. On some occasions, people will offer themselves spontaneously. More often, you'll have to venture out to find them. One of the preconditions is that you're not afraid of being vulnerable and to share your flaws and needs. By intensifying the change process, we mean ensuring that people who were initially less enthused will get on board along the way. In literature this is referred to as the 'tipping point': Suddenly stragglers get excited to join.

- **Set**: When we develop new behavior, our brain circuitry changes. Carefully at first; if you stop your new activity, you will swiftly lose the new connection and your brain will go its merry old way. It's therefore pivotal to mindfully maintain course for a good while.

Over time, this will ensure farm tracks turn into highways. And a new habit will then become embedded in our brain. Scientists say it takes about three months for this to happen. However, this requires regular (if not daily) attention!

The chart on the next page will help you apply the change formula:

## CHANGE FORMULA ITINERARY

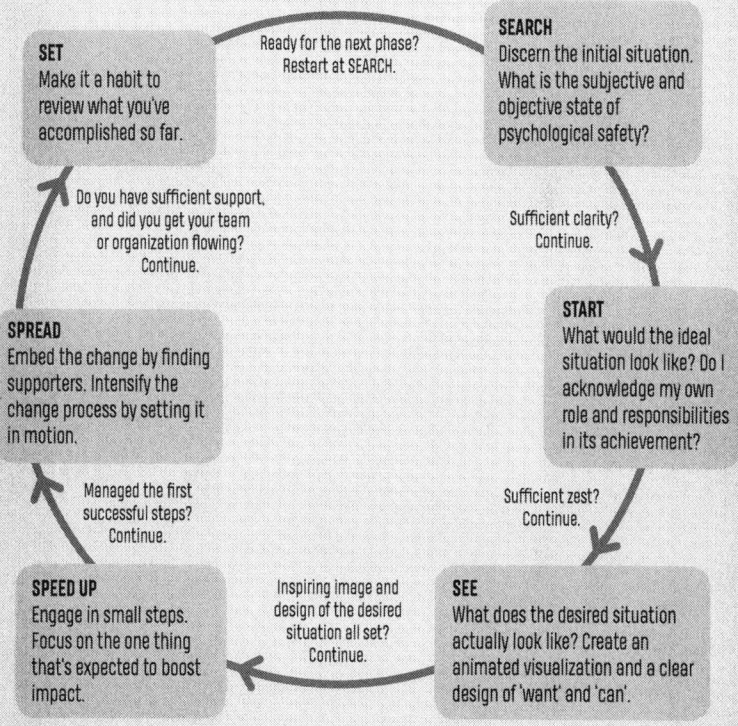

Do you recognize the cold and warm route to psychological safety in your organization? How does leadership influence this process? And how can it be boosted?

'It's your job to convince me I was wrong. Don't be afraid to rebut, be fearless. Make me listen.'

– Steve Jobs

(conversation with an employee after discovering a mistake)

# 6

# HOW TO SPARK SAFETY

Where do you start to cultivate a climate of psychological safety? We would say: At the very beginning. Make sure you *really* want it, and that the three golden ingredients – trust, candor and making a difference – are *on point*. Ideally combined with the change formula from Chapter 5.

By means of the three ingredients, we will walk you through a considerable number of necessary toolkits in the next couple of pages. Please beware: As we address all three ingredients separately, it may seem as though they are unconnected when actually they are closely intertwined. When we spoke of authentic leadership in the last chapter, we found that authenticity is an important bonding agent to manifest the strong interdependence.

Authenticity results in reliability (and with it instills trust), credibility (and with it inspires candor), and recognition (a base for making a difference). Just like the Three Musketeers, however invisible their ties, they come as a package deal: All for one and one for all!

Make sure you keep in mind that working on one ingredient will automatically affect the others. In some ways, all three ingredients could be considered control dials, used to fine-tune your tailored recipe for psychological safety. The chart below illustrates the most important knobs to turn in order to stimulate a climate of fearless performance:

## KNOBS TO TURN

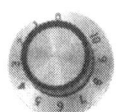  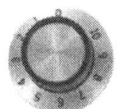

| **Trust** | **Candor** | **Make a difference** |
|---|---|---|
| Interconnection | Autonomy | Very Important Ambition |
| Shared meaning | Self confidence | Focus on essence |
| Common framework | Radical frankness | Learn every day |

## A Grip on Trust

Why do people have the courage to jump out of an airplane? Because they trust the instructor and the parachute on their backs. Why does a Formula-1 driver have the nerve to exit the pitstop and rejoin the circuit at full speed? Because he blindly trusts his mechanics and material. Trust is a form of positive energy that goes hand in hand with the expectation that everything will ultimately work out. Even in the toughest conditions, the hardest times. Building trust never follows universal patterns. However, there are a few practical rules of thumb that will get you a long way: Interconnect, create shared purpose, and establish a common framework.

*Interconnect*

It seems like a no-brainer, but it's often overlooked in practice: To achieve results together, you need to connect. Express your interest in and care for one another. Try not to keep things 'purely professional' and get down to business right away, focusing on performance only; take some time for each other. Try to find out what motivates the other person. What were the key moments in their life? What qualities are they most proud of? What's their aim in life? What do they believe in? Ask more questions if need be. Be aware of that one objective: Connect, and build trust.

> **TOOLKIT TO INTERCONNECT**
>
> - Connection starts with you: Be authentic. Show your true colors. Bring all of you into the conversation, reveal your strengths and limitations.
> - Be self-conscious and try not to make yourself taller or smaller, do not give in to the urge of wanting to be liked.
> - Minimize hierarchic and 'power-driven' behavior (headstrong, propensity for superiority, impulsive, lacking empathy). Select people who can roll with the punches.
> - Be present: Don't clutter your mind with other thoughts, focus on the conversation.
> - Listen well and avoid interrupting the other as much as you can. Make sure you understand before being understood.
> - Allow each other some space, be curious of what moves the other person, and try to make the conversation an interaction.
> - Hold up a mirror, or ask each other challenging questions.
>
> **Beware**: Doing the opposite of these guidelines is the quickest way to disconnect and feed mistrust.

### *Create Shared Meaning*

We don't just fly off and do things. We want our efforts to be meaningful. To be able to inject and eject energy. Alongside connecting, shared significance builds psychological safety and trust, together defining what it means to belong to a team or organization. For example, to what extent do people derive their views, behavior and identity from the group? What are their shared ambitions, individual roles and responsibilities?

> **TOOLKIT TO CREATE SHARED MEANING**
>
> - Make psychological safety recognizable. Explore its importance and substance. Regularly evaluate what it means to you (and the group) and why you are working on it. Create clarity. Relate its meaning to the team or organization vision and performance objectives.
> - Place all attention for psychological safety and the three ingredients in a positive light; don't push it as mandatory. Draw a parallel with the way families interact.
> - Translate desires to change in a strong ambition; visualize ideal future circumstances.
> - Talk about what everyone can contribute individually to create a safer climate.
> - Cast a wider net over psychological safety; besides work, include the home situation in your considerations.
> - Dwell on the meaning and importance of psychological safety at regular intervals – preferably daily.
>
> **TIP**: One IT company decided to install three colored buttons in the meeting room. Pressing the red button meant the situation was considered unsafe, blue was neutral, and green indicated a safe environment.

## *Establish Common Frameworks*

Trust flourishes within anticipated expectation patterns. To minimize mistrust and bolster trust, you need joint frameworks and behavioral guidelines such as values, standards and codes of conduct. Create collective rituals and routines. Make good arrangements. Go the extra mile to make behavior consistent. This way, you're able to fall back on them during decision-making processes and implementations.

> **TOOLKIT FOR COMMON FRAMEWORKS**
>
> - Offer clear boundaries; psychological safety is never a free pass for boundless behavior.
> - Frames ensure consistency, predictability, and with that, safety.
> - Derive these frames from a vision and values at an organizational and personal level. Together, determine what's 'normal'.
> - Implement the frames: Identify what behavior is desirable and undesirable ('This is how we do things here').
> - Make the frames visible to everyone. Use them in every interaction. Point out positive behavior and address negative behavior.
> - See to it that everyone understands your agreements are binding, linking them to consequences.

## A Grip on Candor

Candid comment demonstrates you care about the other person. It means you have the courage to tell the truth. How others respond when you address them, refute them and challenge them depends on the climate of psychological safety in a group. You'll notice and feel this the moment you set foot in a group. Do you sense a prevailing open and cheerful vibe? Or do they gaze as if they're a million miles away; do your words crash into a wall of silence. Do you feel the main point isn't mentioned and stays under the surface? Do the same individuals take the floor time and again, or is everyone alert and excited to get into it? Do they dare contradict each other *and* their boss?

### *Show Autonomy*

Candor expresses exactly what psychological safety is all about: 'being free' and 'having the courage' to speak up. To address others. To stand up for others when you think they are being unfairly excluded. To go against the grain. This is only possible when you feel autonomous. When you make your own choices and take matters into your own hands.

> **TOOLKIT TO SHOW AUTONOMY**
>
> - Pursue your own ambitions and goals.
> - Show personal leadership.
> - Tell your own story.
> - Feel responsible for your own choices, try not to 'dive'.
> - Do not automatically conform to existing rules.
> - Dare to go against the flow.
> - Do not avoid conflict.
> - Denounce 'Calimera Behavior'. Be keen on any kind of dependence, name it, and address people about such behavior.
> - Do not confuse autonomy with an 'anything goes' mentality. Autonomy means that you look for your own possibilities within given contexts and frameworks.

*Show Self-Confidence*

Candor is also a matter of self-confidence. By this we mean the belief in one's own ability, but also a feeling of self-esteem. So self-confidence is always about 'skill' and 'dignity'. Below you will find a number of options to work on self-confidence.

## TOOLKIT FOR SHOWING SELF-CONFIDENCE

- Balance 'skill' and 'dignity'.
- Develop a positive self-image.
- Develop skills by challenging yourself.
- Strengthen belief in your own abilities by asking others for feedback.
- Look at yourself realistically.
- Try to show resilience when you are faced with criticism.
- Try to stay 'cool' when the pressure increases.
- Spot the multiple fibs you tell yourself to avoid confrontation: No time, not my responsibility, almost retired, I don't want to take the blame in case this escalates, they'll never change, not the right time, etc.
- Address one another in the moment. Identify the positive, as well as the negative. Make sure communication is positive and respectful: Directed at behavior and the person.
- Do not dwell on how it will appear if you address something. Do not fear coming across as patronizing, pedantic, smug or directive. As long as you act consciously and with full conviction, go for it!
- Set a good example yourself. Ask to be addressed frankly. Show you can take criticism and what you do with it.
- Encourage others to reflect on their own behavior as much as possible. During meetings, request someone (or the whole team) to observe what happens, then review according to a few fixed criteria. Don't go easy on yourself and take your share of comments.

### Be Radically Candid

Candor has nothing to do with hierarchy. Be candid in all directions: Upwards, sideways, downwards. Don't be afraid to poke and provoke people. And be prepared and ready to provide feedback.

> **TOOLKIT TO BE RADICALLY CANDID**
> 
> - Dare to come out with open-mindedness and positive intention.
> - Be honest about what you think.
> - Actively ask others for feedback.
> - Dare to be vulnerable and ask others for help.
> - Have the courage to give others prompt feedback.
> - Always focus on learning and improving yourself.
> - Be receptive to different opinions and new ideas.
> - Be attentive to blind spots and 'group-think'.
> - Encourage people to have a mind of their own, to be bold enough to be defiant, and to take the initiative. To be able to choose your own stance in any circumstance is the ultimate freedom.
> - Welcome challenges, errors and issues. Help people take small steps towards more autonomy and self-confidence. Or allow one or more team members to support them.
> - Expect candor to lead to (cultural) friction.
> - Stay light on your feet, never too rigid, candor thrives in an open and playful environment.
> - Candor is not a free pass to be unnecessarily tough or hurtful. Try to have a positive impact on the other person. Be (radically) frank and transparent, without deliberately wanting to 'flub' someone's life.

> - Encourage the expression of emotions so you know what the other person feels and thinks.
> - Connect before you offer feedback. Acknowledge any responsibility in the development of the situation.
> - Don't wrap criticism in fake compliments, don't use sandwich tactics (two positive messages versus one negative).
> - Check whether your feedback lands with the other person as you intended.

## A Grip on Making a Difference

Making a difference is an important factor when it comes to psychological safety for two reasons. Firstly, because the will to make a difference helps to build an environment of fearless performance. It is the 'joie de vivre' of psychological safety. It boosts energy, leads to the willingness to learn together and to do everything possible to move forward. Second, making a difference is also an incentive to view psychological safety not as an end, but a means: To make a difference and achieve what you set out to do together. The drive to make a difference starts choosing and pursuing a Very Important Ambition. You try to visualize your ambition and reflect on how to achieve them. Pursuing Very Important Ambitions is not only an excellent way to focus on the essences, but also for targeted learning on a daily basis.

*Very Important Ambition*

Making a difference starts with choosing a Very Important Ambition (VIA). A final destination that you want to reach at all costs. Not because you have to, but because you want to. An ambition that enables you to have an impact. The toolkit below lists a number of interventions to achieve such a VIA.

> **TOOLKIT TO PURSUE A VERY IMPORTANT AMBITION**
> - Assume, as much as possible 'wanting' and not 'must' do.
> - Assume that not everything is equally important to you/your life.
> - Consider where you want to have the most impact (where do you want to be a 'leverage'?).
> - Define a higher purpose. Reflect on your own objective. What is your end game? What makes your heart tick?
> - Visualize the ambition and the (intermediate) goal in a vivid way, so that everyone has the same image of what matters.
> - Name and visualize the obstacles that will be overcome.
> - Name and visualize 'battles' to be won.
> - Share your promise. Verbalize a value proposition. What promises will you make? What will you produce, deliver or achieve? What results can you be held accountable for?
> - Specify the skills and competence you need to realize your ambition.
> - Translate that ambition into concrete and time-determined (intermediate) goals.

*Focusing on The Essence*

Making a difference is not only a matter of pursuing Very Important Ambitions, but also of focusing on the essence. Concentrate on what is important to you. But also: design a motivational scoreboard, so that you know how you are doing. And discuss progress regularly Research shows that measuring and discussing progress is one of the most powerful motivators. What if the scores indicate no progress has been made? Rethink your activities. Look for alternative options. Then show flexibility and take a different approach.

> **TOOLKIT TO FOCUS ON THE ESSENCE**
>
> - Get started as soon as possible and take a step forward every day.
> - Concentrate on what is important to you. Shield yourself from unnecessary stimuli.
> - Get rid of unnecessary ballast.
> - Measure progress: Develop your own team scoreboard.
> - Use each other's strengths and encourage their development.
> - Regularly review progress together to prevent a good track record from fading. What went well? What made things go better? What did we do differently? Who contributed what in this process? Who came up with the idea to do things differently?
> - Employ the 'scaling question' during these conversations to evaluate achievements on a scale of one to ten. Use one or more indicators to show you are on the right track. Dispel aversion towards or fear of tracking and measuring. It's not about checking people, but about gathering information to learn from.

- Point out that to be successful in computer games, players mostly rely on real-time information they receive. You get more energized when you know the score.
- Be critical and sharp at meetings: Try not to relativize or trivialize inadequate performance. Avoid the guilt trip, and prevent the pot from calling the kettle black.
- If things don't work out the way you'd hoped, take a step back. Find out exactly what's going on, think up an alternative way to get to the objective, get started, ensure support and review if this *does* work. Sounds familiar? Yep, these are the distinct phases of the change formula from Chapter 5.

### *Learn Every Day*

Finally, don't just make progress, but learn every day. Provide a climate of learning, learning and learning again. Only then is it possible to operate in a vital environment of psychological security. Do you want to know more about best ways and practical methods to learn to stimulate a climate of psychological safety? Read the Field Guide on Psychological Safety that will be soon published in English. You can also visit the English part of our website www.psychological-safety.net.

## Three Flight Routes to Create *Safe Zones*

We're almost there. We've explained what psychological safety is and how it emerges, we've told you about the lay of the land in companies, about undermining forces, and how to change the tide towards safer environments. In this chapter we've provided you with a good number of tips and tricks to support you in your daily practice. All the while underlining the fact that the three golden ingredients should be seen in conjunction, not as separate entities. It's not a matter of trust *or* candor *or* making a difference, but of the *golden* combination. In that light, the subtitle of our book is somewhat misleading. It's not just about cultivating candid teams, it's just as much about building trusting teams that make a difference. But it'd make the subtitle a tad lengthy...

Coming to the end of this book, we're giving you three approaches to optimize psychological safety: The procedural, the cultural and the interplay route. Each with their own place in the continuum from 'hard' to 'soft'.

### POSITION OF FLIGHT ROUTES IN THE CHANGE CONTINUUM

| Procedural Route | Cultural Route | Interplay Route |
|---|---|---|

**HARD APPROACH** — **SOFT APPROACH**

## The Procedural Route

Keeping an airplane in the air seems primarily a question of technique and laws of nature. But flying is also human work. And humans make mistakes, especially without the right climate of psychological safety. In March 1977, two jumbo jets collided on the runway in Tenerife. Investigations into the tragedy, which killed 583 people, reported it was caused by human error. Pressured by circumstances – there was a thick fog and the plane had been delayed – the experienced Captain thought he had been cleared for take-off. His Co-pilot doubted his judgement but didn't have the guts to defy his superior officer. So he kept silent...

The tragedy brought to light the extreme hierarchy in aviation in an extremely painful way. In the years after the war, many pilots had switched from the air force to civil aviation. In the cockpit, their word was law. They held a zero-tolerance policy on defiance. Aviation authority analysis revealed that the culture of hierarchy had often played a part in other plane crashes as well. In the aftermath of this particular event, NASA endorsed a program: Crew Resource Management (CRM). It was implemented during the eighties through extensive training programs, including video instructions and print. Today, it's the global standard training program for every airline, with regular refresher courses to safeguard this behavior pattern. What *is* the behavior pattern? Prior to each flight, the cockpit crew goes through the flight plan during the briefing. At the end of each flight, there's a debrief. Between briefing and debrief, a period of special circumstances takes effect: Everyone can, no *has to* contradict, regardless of rank and position. Every single crew member is held responsible. The 'emergency communication plan' is a 3-step component of CRM. Should a co-pilot detect something is amiss, he/she will point out in a non-threatening present-tense form: 'I feel that...' Should this be ignored, a pre-agreed sentence can be used, such as: 'I am not comfortable with...' And as a last resort: 'Stop this procedure!' As soon as someone says this, everyone stops all proceedings. If they've already started descent, they have to call for a go-around.

CRM has become a given in aviation. Psychological safety in aviation has greatly improved as a result. The number of air disasters has – partly due to technical improvements – been reduced to an all-time low. And the approach has since then been 'adopted' by manufacturers, hospital, fire brigades and crisis teams, navigation, nuclear plants and oil rigs. Mostly branches in which people work with advanced technology under a lot of pressure, and according to routine operations. The results are promising, especially when dealing with disaster and crisis situations. Although one has to wonder about the added value of similar programs in workplaces that are not geared towards routine but towards realizing creative expression.

## The Cultural Route

Pixar is the company behind blockbusters such as *Toy Story* and *Finding Nemo*. A company in which people perform under high pressure, working with the most advanced technology currently available. However, unlike in aviation, it's not about routine operations, but about optimizing creativity. Pixar ringleaders do everything in their power to create a culture of sparked safety. Ed Cattmull, former CEO at Pixar, talks about this in his book *Creativity Inc*. 'If you give a good idea to a mediocre team, they will screw it up. If you give a mediocre idea to a brilliant team, they will either fix it or throw it away and come up with something better.' The main goal at Pixar is to ensure the team works. Therefore, most of the attention is focused on building and sustaining group relationships. When interrelationships are good, performance excellence will follow, as everyone knows.

To spark safety, the company follows a number of set rituals. For one, there's the bi-monthly gathering of 'Braintrust', where ongoing movie projects are shown to the most experienced employees in the company – writers, directors, producers, executives – followed by an open discussion with the authors, in which everyone shares feedback with utmost candor. The purpose of the meetings is to push towards excellence; they are not primarily focused on addressing problems or finding solutions.

Afterwards, the authors will hopefully have a different perspective on their work, ultimately improving the final product.

Another ritual is 'Notes Day', when all work is shut down for a day to facilitate brainstorming sessions throughout the entire company, and employees from all sections can submit ideas on how to improve the company. The response is tremendous. Everyone has the potential to be creative, according to Catmull. But most people don't know it themselves. Only when we liberate them of their fears and uncertainties, and offer them a safe environment where they feel free to spitball ideas candidly, can we create a better workplace.

Just like in aviation, rituals stem from past incidents and protuberances. During production of *Toy Story 2*, the pressure was sky high; people burned out and dropped out with physical and mental complaints. One employee even left his baby alone in an overheated car. The rituals were introduced to counteract the Race Teams you read about in Chapter 3. They ensure psychological safety without tampering with the ambition to deliver creative excellence in a wildly competitive environment.

## The Interplay Route

Programs and rituals are a major factor in psychological safety. However, they are insufficient for trust, candor and making a difference to permeate deep into the heart of teams and organizations. This is where the daily interaction between human beings comes into play. Jitske Kramer uses a term that rocks well in this context. 'Jamming': Making music together through improvisation. It lifts you out of your comfort zone and helps you create a sound of your own while adapting to the sound of others. You can fly solo and step back in line. The end result is inherently uncertain.

To interplay or jam means you are open to variation, new opportunities and experiences. To have the guts to experiment like you've never done before. To be in it, heart and soul, and create magical moments. Interaction also means you know when to allow room for others. It places high demands on people. Like the courage to show yourself. To let go of existing securities, and embrace the uncertainty of adventure.

> The results are promising, especially when dealing with disaster and crisis situations

This could be the greatest paradox of psychological safety: To have to leave behind obvious safety to be able to create new safety. We wish you good luck in these endeavors!

> Do you recognize the relationship between programmatic, ritual and interactive approaches within your organization? What would the optimum combination of flight routes to trust, candor and making a difference be in your opinion?

> If you want to know how you can stimulate psychological safety through an interactive approach, read the accompanying Field Guide Psychological Safety (soon to be published in English). It is packed with tips, recommendations, nudges, example behaviors and ready-made scripts to exercise.

'The range of what we think and do is limited by what we fail to notice. And because we fail to notice that we fail to notice, there is little we can do to change.'

– R.D. Laing

# THE STORY OF JORIENE AND HANS

## Joriene's Story

It all started with that one intern. She was emotionally unstable and unable to attend school, yet still subject to compulsory schooling. The secondary vocational school rep asked if I could place her in my accredited learning company. I didn't know whether I could, but I knew I really wanted to. She taught me something I kind of already knew deep down inside: Every human being wants to be seen. It's a fact of life. Each year, there were more interns who weren't able to find or keep a mainstream internship for a multitude of reasons. I started a foundation. It's because of the adolescents I met through this foundation that I was able to develop my method for cultivating psychological safety. Through trial and error, my feet lodged deep in the mud.

I have used these experiences and my knowledge to assist all possible kinds of teams and organizations in cultivating a climate of psychological safety. So, you could be tempted to think that the topic is easy as pie to me. Like pulling a rabbit from a hat. On the contrary. I'm constantly reminded of how hard a topic it is to work on. How much people grapple with it, myself included. Because I myself am part of the process.

To me psychological safety is all about being confident and gaining confidence of your raison d'être as a person. It's about being allowed space to display and deploy your authentic self. Without compromising at the risk of losing your own self. So you can leave your mark in other people's lives, as well as your own.

Maturing into authenticity is a journey of peaks and troughs. The same goes for me. I remember a time when I was a Junior Consultant on a project for a client whose basic values were not in line with my own. As a consequence, going to work used to be pure agony for me. I didn't have the guts to talk about it with my colleagues; they were so senior and experienced; they had written books and managed large international projects. Who was I to call anything into question? Let alone the proven approach they had developed? I ended up crying at my client's office. And then I quit my job and branched out on my own. Gradually, I felt the need to connect with peers. At first, it seemed like a positive development, but then I found candor and trust were lacking. Not only did it leave a scar, it also led to trust issues.

And now there's a book. Out of the blue. Because I commented on Hans' blog. We spoke on the phone, went for a coffee, and it all pieced together. Sounds amazing, right? And so it is. Yet the struggle with psychological safety continues. It's part of the various, sometimes paradoxical roles I have. My feet lodged in the mud with the youngsters, and at the same time standing on the sidelines as an observer. Working with my employees, building my own trust, so they have the guts to be open and honest. While I also have my own thoughts – that I don't always keep to myself. The struggle is also in confronting myself. My less beautiful aspects. Aspects I coach other people on. It is also in allowing my children room to develop into who they are. Accepting my husband handles disappointment differently, and that it's okay that he does. And accepting this is not always easy for me. Placing myself in a vulnerable position, and simultaneously embracing myself and the other. Phew...

The entire process, the varying roles and corresponding struggles, it makes me larger than life and humbles me all at once.

## Hans' Story

Contrary to Joriene's world, the concept of psychological safety has always been a faint hum in mine. I had heard people talk about it but couldn't quite grasp what it was all about. Partly because I have been straddling the border, since I care to remember, always the odd man out, displaced. Literally because I was born in a foreign country, growing up in an international setting. The country I lived in at the time considered foreigners (a word still allowed in the last century) to be outsiders. And my homeland was so unfamiliar to me, that it too felt alien. Once I settled in the Netherlands, part of that feeling disappeared. But never to the point of being right at home.

In fact, unwittingly there were also advantages to profiling myself as an outcast. Although the people I depended on – teachers at first, then professors and later executives – appreciated my input, they didn't have a hold on me. 'You're a real maverick,' a manager once told me. 'You provide a creative twist.' Upon which he told the group in no uncertain words there was only room for one left-winger. That was me. It became like a game to me to expand my position of candor. I actually continued to live in various worlds: I took part, but was part of something else at the same time. I was simultaneously a scientist and a professional drummer. I was a loyal employee and doing a thousand-and-one things on the side. Why? Because it turned into a habit. Because it felt good. And because it gave me a certain status.

My tipping point came when I read Robert Musil's voluminous novel *The Man without Qualities* during an extended period of illness. It tells the story of a young mathematician who has dissociated from society. He may well have known how to easily adapt to various social layers, but in time this leads to a loss of personality. As soon as I finished reading the book, I knew: From now on, I would follow suit. Fit in. Make a difference.

In recent years, this has led to a constant flow of activities and books, all related to energetic change and innovation. And that's where the concept of psychological safety came into play. Exploring new stuff is not a question of going solo, but interplay. Best served on a plate of psychological safety. This book is living proof of that.

A few months ago, Joriene and I had never met. The book was written in a flow bordering magic. Since then, I've come to know it has nothing to do with magic, but psychological safety. I will keep this in mind as long as I may live.

# FREQUENTLY ASKED QUESTIONS

We're almost there. By now, you know what psychological safety is, how it works and how you can put it to practice. Hopefully, it makes sense and already sounds somewhat familiar to you. Maybe you've marked some passages to reread at a later stage (as we're in the habit of doing...). Maybe you left some exclamation marks in the margin. Or a question mark, because you couldn't quite grasp what was being said, or because you wanted to noodle on it some more. In an attempt to help you on your way, we've answered a few commonly heard questions below; starting with questions relating to content, then passing on to questions about the process. Should your particular question not be answered, feel free to visit our web site **www.psychological-safety.net** where you'll find more information related to the subject. Not able to find what you're looking for there either? Send us a message, we're be happy to provide you with more details.

Since it's all about building psychological safety, with this code **BPV-HLJB-1220** you get 3-month access to the members' part of our website for FREE.

Go to www.psychological-safety.net/members and be inspired by nudges, scripts, sheets and more. All to pave the way to perform fearlessly.

## Content-Related Questions

*How do you handle the fact that psychological safety is fleshed out differently by different individuals?*

We wouldn't give it too much thought. Psychological safety is a multi-dimensional concept. Meaning it's all about 'both-and' (times five, as there are five dimensions). When you talk about psychological safety, you have both a wide range and a guiding framework at your disposal. When you start working on psychological safety, try to stick to the framework. Focus on things directly related to psychological safety. But be careful not to be too rigid when things are put forward that put you and your team or organization in a position to make a difference. In the end, psychological safety is not a purpose in itself but a means to make a positive impact.

*Does psychological safety also benefit a technical IT company? Isn't it more of a non-profit or municipal thing?*

That's a question we often hear. One where the branch that supposedly doesn't qualify for psychological safety can be filled in at will. Let's clarify this once and for all: Psychological safety is about people, not about branches. Where people are at work, psychological safety is a prerequisite to good collaboration. To optimally tap into your collective potential. So yes, it's also suitable for an IT company – if that company wants to make a difference. Also, to rid the whole concept of 'soft' connotations, we've lined our book with examples of tough, data-driven enterprises like Amazon and Google. The way you reflect on psychological safety can differ from one company or team to another. The foundation remains: Psychological safety results from trust + candor + making a difference.

*Is diversity tantamount to psychological safety?*

No, but they are clearly linked. Diversity refers to a cocktail of people causing teams to be more creative and better performing. If you really want to exploit diversity, you need to go the extra mile. You'll need to make people feel seen and like they belong. This is called 'inclusivity'. Being one of the five (Big Five) dimensions, inclusion is paramount to cultivating a climate of psychological safety, where people operate on an equal basis.

*Ever since we've put psychological safety on our agenda, I feel less safe rather than the other way around. Is that weird?*

For starters, feelings are never weird. They are here to show you something important. In fact, there are most probably people around you who share your feelings. This is not to say that you have to share private issues 'for the sake of' psychological safety, just to show mutual trust and candor. That doesn't make sense. If you don't feel comfortable to talk about private stuff, then don't. It would feel unsafe if you would. Be vigilant of things that are introduced as the 'new normal' under the guise of psychological safety. Psychological safety 'on the agenda' reeks of a formal management approach; one that jeopardizes the objective in our view. Psychological safety refers to culture and a way of collaborating. It's not something that should feature on some agenda. It's something you talk about. Something you decide on. And most of all, something you *do*.

## Process-Related Questions

*Where do I start when I want to improve psychological safety in my team?*

A very clear-cut question that generally proves harder to answer. It depends a lot on the context and personalities within a team and organization. What exactly is at play? What dynamics can be distinguished in the team or the organization? What distinctive patterns? What are the culture and energy status of the team? What about your interpretation and compliance with regards to the five dimensions of psychological safety? Did the drive to do 'something' with regards to this topic come from within, or was it dictated from up top or outside? Is the situation clear-cut or rather complex and tough? For this reason, in our 6S Formula, we've stressed the importance of a search phase in which to assess the situation properly first. What do you see happening around you? What signals are pointing towards (un)safety? What are the thoughts on this subject within the group? You can start an open conversation about this or use a questionnaire for example (which you can find on psychologischeveiligheid.net). Such conversations are never non-committal. They are interventions to set people's minds at work. The transformation starts with the first question. Psychological safety can't be implemented systematically; it's something you cultivate, step by step, always in the here and now. All the while keeping it as light and breezy as possible. Use energizing techniques such as '1-2-4-all' (Liberating Structures). Allow people room to think about a question or statement, and subsequently to talk about it in twos to come to a collective answer. Repeat the same process in fours and eventually as a group. It's not only energizing, it also leads to trust and candor.

***Do you have to score well on all 'Big Five' elements?***
Our answer here is somewhat double. It's not our intention to propel either one of the five dimensions as the core of psychological safety. Quite frequently, our work brings us to organizations that proudly talk about their unique vibe of 'inclusion' and their 'innovative climate'. To us, it's more of an incentive to ask about the state of the other dimensions. On the other hand, we understand it's important to set priorities. Working on all five dimensions at the same time is over the top and by no means always as effective. Again, it all depends on context and your specific ambitions. All the while making sure not to neglect the other dimensions.

***All that talking and working on a climate of psychological safety, doesn't that take way too long and require way too much of my time?***
Behavioral change doesn't have to take long at all. It only takes a few weeks to months for the first results to be discernable. As long as you make sure you take the context into account, paint a crystal clear (and collective) picture of what you want to achieve, and start experimenting without delay. It's a scientific fact. The 6S model is deeply rooted in scientific research about effective and efficient behavioral change. Why then does it take so long in practice, and sometimes to no avail? Because we don't draw lessons from what science teaches us. Because we often do exactly the opposite of what we're meant to do.

Because executives say one thing (how important psychological safety is to them), and then turn around and do the exact opposite (not make time for it). We don't want to embellish the situation: Of course it takes time to work on psychological safety. But the time invested will recoup itself twice over in the long run (not meaning years, but weeks or months).

### *When working on psychological safety, what are the most common mistakes?*

In our books, the number one by far is paying attention to psychological safety because it's being hyped. This generally leads to superficial copies of success cases elsewhere. Once the novelty wears off, it's on to the next hype. Our number two: The strategic approach. Complicated analyses, impressive action and step-by-step plans, mandatory training sessions deployed on a large scale, staff – or worse: A Chief Safety Officer – to propagate the Gospel of safety, and so on and so forth. The outcome: Too much talk and not enough action. Number three is the opposite: Start haphazardly without taking the time to thoroughly think things through and prepare. Jumping to conclusions & pulling the trigger. Sure, action is okay, but not when it's unfocused. By the way, can you guess the most common mistake by a longshot? Making all three at once...

# REFERENCES

*p. 11*     The anecdote comes from the book *Bezonomics* by Brian Dumaine (2020), pages 53-54.

*p. 13*     The 85% mentioned is derived from a scientific study from Miliken et al. (2003). The Dutch percentage of 69% is obtained through a survey of the '*Energy of the Working Population in the Netherlands*', commissioned by EnergyFinder in 2008.

*p. 14*     Refer to Edmondson (1999), Edmondson (2003), Edmondson and Mogelof (2005), Edmondson and Harvey (2017), and (Edmondson (2019) for Amy Edmondson's ideology.

*p. 22*     We drew up this paragraph using the following sources: Barling (1996), Fijbes (2017), Frost (2003), Marcha and Verweel (2003), and Schrijvers (2002).

*p. 23*     For further research on the adverse effect of anxiety, refer to: Fijbes (2017) and Keegan (2015).

*p. 25*     The video can be found at *www.youtube.com/watch?v=TNwhIHqM60g*.

*p. 25*     For more information on Eisenstat's experiments, refer to: Sutherland (2014), Thun (2019), and *www.joelonsoftware.com/2005/07/25/hitting-the-high-notes/*. The experimental studies that Eisenstat conducted can be traced back to a strong tradition.

As early as 1968, three Americans published a white paper on the remarkable individual differences between programmers. The fastest programmers were said to perform 25 times faster than the slowest. See: Sackman et al (1968). In the course of this century, it became widely accepted to refer to them as 'tenx coders' (working ten times faster).

*p. 25*  On the elasticity of human performance, refer to: Hansen (2018), Keller and Price (2011), Salas et al (2005), and Shaw (2017).

*p. 26*  For a good description of the Google work culture, refer to: Bock (2015) and Schmidt & Rosenberg (2014).

*p. 28*  C. Duhigg describes the research process in the NYT Magazine article titled *What Google Learned From Its Quest to Build the Perfect Team*, dated 25 February 2016.

*p. 29*  The list and scenarios described later on have been found on Google's 're:work' site. There's more material on psychological safety in teams on this site. See: *https://rework.withgoogle.com/guides/understanding-team-effectiveness/steps/introduction/*.

*p. 48*  The hostage crisis described here was found in Kohlrieser (2012). In this book, he elaborates on the lessons leaders can draw from it. In Kohlrieser (2006), there's more information on the dynamics of hostage situations.

*p. 53* Candor is a somewhat classical term, mostly used in literature and Biblical references, and less common nowadays. It's often replaced by the term 'bold' or 'daring' in English. Though not entirely wrong, it surpasses the richer connotations linked with the term 'candid'. Apart from bravery, courage and fearlessness, candor also refers to traits such as an open mind, frankness and freedom, i.e. independence.

*p. 54* Watch the video at *www.youtube.com/watch?v=C-JXnYMl_SuA*.

*p. 57* The anecdote is a combination of our experience and the events described in the book *High Impact Teaming* by Stefan DeCuyper et al (2019).

*p. 60* To read more on the nature, workings and effects of energy, refer to Hans van der Loo and Patrick Davidson (2019).

*p. 61* EnergyFinder is a measuring instrument used to identify the energy within teams and organizations. Since 2014, we've also measured the energy of the working population in the Netherlands among over 5,000 employees. The database is derived from this data.

*p. 61* For more information on the Measure of Psychological Safety, refer to: Edmondson (2019), p213-215.

*p. 61* The Psychological Safety Index (PSI) referred to in this chapter is based on existing data. Meanwhile, we've also performed dedicated research on psychological safety in the Netherlands, and the results show great similarity (the last measurement carried out in the midst of the Covid-19 pandemic – April 2020 – reveals a slightly lower index of 51%).

*p. 63* The four zones are the result of a division into two dimensions: The quantity of energy (amount or intensity) that can vary from low to high, and the quality of energy, varying from negative (pessimistic, passive and hardly cooperative) to positive (enthusiastic, inspired and prepared to cooperate extensively). Research shows that the two dimensions are independent of each other. For more information and scientific support of this classification, refer to: Bruch and Vogel (2011), Van der Loo and Davidson (2019), Van der Zwan (2017).

*p. 78* Recent examples of books on 'happy culture' and 'happiness at work' are: Geurts (2019) and Mes & Peper (2018).

*p. 79* The WWR report can be downloaded at *www.wrr.nl/publicaties/rapporten/2020/01/15/het-betere-werk*.

*p. 80* For an inspiring and insightful book on the 'culture of fear', we refer you to Fijbes (2017).

*p. 81* The term 'scaredy-lion' is translated from the Dutch word angsthaan, which we borrowed from Inge Mink. She has written multiple articles on this subject for the management site, such as: *www.managementsite.nl/angsthanen-mt*.

*p. 82* For a scientifically substantiated essay on the negative effects of inner demons and fears, refer to: Tierney and Baumeister (2019).

*p. 84* This phenomenon is also known as the 'Thomas Theorem'. It was first documented in a 1928 study named *The Child in America: Behavior problems and programs*. The principle served to underpin the self-fulfilling prophecy, where the prediction alone makes it come true.

*p. 85* In the WWR report mentioned earlier (see p. 79), there are numerous examples and studies of aggressive client behavior towards professional aid workers.

*p. 87* In academia, the debate on whether negative emotions are three, four or five times more powerful than positive is still ongoing. We chose the middle ground – in this case four. Research on the 'positivity ratio' – the balance between positive and negative emotions – was conducted by the American psychologist Barbara Fredrickson (2009) inter alia.

*p. 95* The anecdote mentioned here was borrowed from Daniel Coyle (2018).

*p. 96* Jim Edwards: Google employees confess all the things they hated most about working at Google. Business Insider, 12 December 2016. See: *www.businessinsider.nl/google-employees-worstthings-about-working-at-google-2016-12?international= true&r=US*.

*p. 100* In his book *Leaders Eat Last*, Simon Sinek has some commendable remarks about the relationship between leadership and creating what he calls 'safe circles'.

*p. 123* The topic 'progress-oriented work' has been described in a scientifically substantiated and at the same time practical fashion by Coert Visser (2016, 2017, 2018).

*p. 126* For a detailed explanation of 'Crew Resource Management' and other measures in aviation to increase psychological safety, refer to: Suzanne Gordon et al (2013). Van Lonkhuyzen (2015) also has some interesting comments on the importance of overruling in the cockpit.

*p. 128* The rituals cherished at Pixar have been described in detail by Ed Catmull (2014) in his book *Creativity, Inc.*

*p. 130* For an inspiring discourse on 'jamming', refer to: Jitske Kramer (2019). Jaap Boonstra (2018) has written a thorough book on establishing interplay.

# LITERATURE

- Ardon, A. (2018). *Break the Cycle! How managers block change without realizing it,* Amsterdam/Antwerp: Business Contact.
- Barling, J. (1996). *The Prediction, Experience and Consequences of Workplace Violence.* Washington D.C: American Psychological Association.
- Bergeijk, J. van (2019). *Binnen bij bol.com. Undercover bij de winkel van ons allemaal (Inside Bol.com. Undercover at the shop around the corner),* Amsterdam: Querido Fosfor.
- Bock, L. (2015). *Work Rules!: Insights from Inside Google That Will Transform How You Live and Lead.* Amsterdam: Ambo/Anthos Uitgevers.
- Boonstra, J. (2018). Organizational Change as Collaborative Play. A positive view on change and innovation in organizations. Deventer: Vakmedianet.
- Bruch, H. & B. Vogel (2011). *Fully Charged. How Great Leaders Boost Their Organization's Energy and Ignite High Performance.* Boston: Harvard Business Review.
- Catmull, E. (2014). *Creativity. Inc. Overcoming the Unseen Forces That Stand in the Way of True Inspiration.* New York City: Random House.

- Clark, T. (2020). *The 4 Stages of Psychological Safety*. Oakland: Berrett-Koehler Publishers.
- Covey, S. (2006). *The Speed of Trust. The One Thing That Changes Everything*. New York City: Simon & Schuster.
- Coyle, D. (2018). *The Culture Code. The Secrets of Highly Successful Groups*. New York City: Bantam Books.
- De Cuyper, S., E. Raes & A. Boon (2019). *High Impact Teaming. Bewust, effectief, efficiënt samenwerken*. Amsterdam/Antwerpen: Business Contact.
- Dumaine, B. (2020). *Bezonomics. How Amazon is changing our lives, and what the world's best companies are learning from it*. New York City: Simon & Schuster Ltd.
- Edmondson, A. (1999). *Psychological Safety and Learning Behavior in work Teams*. Administrative Science Quarterly, 350-383.
- Edmondson, A. (2003). *Managing the Risk of Learning. Psychological Safety in Work Teams*. In: International Handbook of Organizational Teamwork and Cooperative Working (p. 255-276). London: Blackwell.
- Edmondson, A. & J.P. Mogelof (2005). *Explaining Psychological Safety in Innovation Teams. Organizational Culture, Team Dynamics or Personality?* In: Creativity and Innovation in Organizational Teams (p. 109-136). Mahwah NJ: Lawrence Erlbaum Associate Press.

- Edmondson, A. & J.F. Harvey (2017). *Extreme Teaming. Lessons in Complex, Corss-Sector leadership*. Bingley: Emerald Publishing.
- Edmondson, A. (2019). *The Fearless Organization. Creating Psychological Safety in the Workplace for Learning, Innovation and Growth*. Hoboken NJ: John Wiley & Sons.
- EnergyFinder (2018). *De energie van werkend Nederland 2014 – 2018 (Energy Levels of the Working Population in the Netherlands)*. Amsterdam: Energy Finder.
- Fijbes, P. (2017). *Angstcultuur. Krijg grip op angst in organisaties (Corporate Culture of Fear. How to get a grip on fear within organizations)*. Amsterdam: Boom uitgevers.
- Fredrickson, B. (2009). *Positivity – Discover the upward spiral that will change your life*. New York City: Penguin Random House.
- Frost, P.J. (2003). *Toxic Emotions at Work. How Compassionate Managers Handle Pain and Conflict*. Boston: Harvard Business School Press.
- Geurts, R. (2019). *De gelukkige organisatie. Organisatieontwikkeling vanuit betekenis (The Happy Organization. Meaningful organizational development)*. Amsterdam: Boom uitgevers.
- Gordon, S., P. Mendenhall & B. O'Connor (2013). *Beyond the Checklist. What Else Healthcare Can Learn from Aviation Teamwork and Safety*. New York City: Cornwell University Press.

- Hansen, M.T. (2018). *Great at Work. How Top Performers Do Less, Work Better, and Achieve More*. New York City: Simon & Schuster.
- Harvey, J.B. (1974). *The Abilene Paradox: The Management of Agreement*. Organizational Dynamics, 63-80.
- Heins, G. (2017). *Aanspreken? Gewoon doen!. Hoe je nou écht een aanspreekcultuur creëert (Addressing People? Just Do It! How to really create a culture of justification)*. Amsterdam: Boom Uitgevers.
- Kahn, W.A. (1990). *Psychological Conditions of Personal Engagement and Disengagement at Work*. Academy of Management Journal, 692-724.
- Keegan, S.M. (2015). *The Psychology of Fear in Organizations. How to Transform anxiety into Well-Being, Productivity and Innovation*. London: Kogan Page.
- Keller, S. & C. Price. (2011). *Beyond Performance. How Great Organizations Build Ultimate Competitive Advantage*. Hoboken NJ: John Wiley & Sons.
- Kohlrieser, G. (2006). *Hostage at The Table. How Leaders Can Overcome Conflict, Influence Others, and Raise Performance*. San Francisco: Jossey Bass.
- Kohlrieser, G. (2012). *Care to Dare. Unleashing Astonishing Potential Through Secure Base Leadership*. Chichester: John Wiley & Sons.
- Kramer, J. (2019). *Jam Cultures. Over inclusie: meedoen, meepraten, meebeslissen (Jam Cultures. On inclusion: participation, conversation, decision-making)*. Deventer: Management Impact.

- Laloux, F. (2014). *Reinventing Organizations*. Eastbourne: Gardners Books.
- Lonkhuyzen, P. van (2015). *Tegenspraak. Hoe je beter wordt van dwarsliggers (Contradiction. How to get better through obstructionism)*. Zaltbommel: Uitgeverij Haystack.
- Loo, H. van der & P. Davidson. (2019). *Werkvuur. Hoe energieke mensen en teams positieve impact maken (Working Fire. How energetic people and teams inspire positive impact)*. Amsterdam: Boom Uitgevers.
- Marcha, V. & P. Verweel (2003). *De cultuur van angst (The Culture of Fear)*. Amsterdam: Uitgeverij SWP.
- Mes, H. & G. Peper (2018). *Employee Experience. Happy People, Better Business*. Alphen aan den Rijn: Vakmedianet.
- Miliken, F.J, E.W. Morrison & P.F. Hewlin (2003). *An Exploratory study of Employee Silence*. Journal of Management Studies, 1453-1476.
- Norcross, J.C. (2012). *Changeology – 5 Steps to Realizing Your Goals and Resolutions*. New York City: Simon & Schuster.
- Prochaska, J.O, J.C. Norcross & C.C. DiClemente (1995). *Changing for Good*. New York City: Avon.
- Radeck. D. & L. Hull. (2018). *Psychological Safety: The Key to Happy, High-performing People and Teams*. The Academy of Brain-based Leadership.

- Sackman, H., W.J. Erikson & E.E. Grant (1968). *Exploratory Experimental Studies Comparing Online and Offline Programming Performance*. Communication of the ACM, 11, 3-11.
- Salas, E., D.E. Sims & C.S. Burke (2005). *Is there a 'Big Five' in Teamwork?* Small Group Research, 36, 555599.
- Scott, K. (2017). *Radicaal openhartig. Wees een baas door mens te blijven (Radical Candor. Be a boss by staying human)*. Amsterdam: Lev.
- Schein, E.H. (1985). *Organizational Culture and Leadership*. New York City: Jossey Bass Wiley.
- Schein, E.H. (1987). *The Clinical Perspective in Field Work*. Thousand Oaks: Sage.
- Schmidt, E. & J. Rosenberg (2017). *How Google Works*. New York City: Amazon.
- Schrijvers, J. (2002). *Hoe word ik een rat? De kunst van het konkelen en samenzweren (How to Rat. The art of platting and scheming)*. Schiedam: Scriptum.
- Shaw, R.B. (2017). *Extreme Teams. Why Pixar, Netflix, AirBnB, and Other Cutting-Edge Companies Succeeded Where Most Fail*. New York City: Amazon
- Sinek, S. (2014). *Leaders Eat Last. Why Some Teams Pull Together and Others Don't*. London: Portfolio Penguin.
- Sutherland, J. (2014). *Scrum – The Art of Doing Twice the Work in Half the Time*. New York City: Crown Business.
- Tierney, J. & R.F. Baumeister. (2020).*The Power of Bad. And How to Overcome It*. London: Allen Lane.

LITERATURE

- Visser, C. (2016). *Progressiegericht werken. Betekenisvolle vooruitgang (Working for Advancement. Meaningful Progress)*. Driebergen-Rijsenburg: Just-in-Time Books.
- Visser, C. (2017). *De psychologie van progressie. Kiezen voor vooruitgang (The Psychology of Advancement. Choosing Progress)*. Driebergen-Rijsenburg: Just-in-Time Books.
- Visser. C. (2018). *Handboek Progressiegericht Coachen (Manual to Working for Advancement)*. Driebergen-Rijsenburg: Just-in-Time Books.
- Zwan, C. van der (2017). *Naar energieke teams. Wat te doen? Als vertragen misschien wel versnellen is (Working on Energetic Teams. How to proceed when slowing down could mean speeding up?)*. Proefschrift VU Amsterdam.

Printed in Poland
by Amazon Fulfillment
Poland Sp. z o.o., Wrocław